D0707756

D. ELUSIONAL
E. NTITLEMENT
D. ISORDER:

*The Unofficial Disease That
Is Destroying America's Spirit*

---

*I Want It Now…
I Want The Best…
I Want It Free…
Somebody Owes Me!*

E. A. SHOCKNEY PhD, LPC

iUniverse, Inc.
New York Bloomington

DELUSIONAL ENTITLEMENT DISORDER:
The Unofficial Disease That Is Destroying America's Spirit
I Want It Now, I Want The Best, I Want
It Free, Somebody Owes Me!

iUniverse books may be ordered through booksellers or by contacting:

iUniverse
1663 Liberty Drive
Bloomington, IN 47403
www.iuniverse.com
1-800-Authors (1-800-288-4677)

Because of the dynamic nature of the Internet, any Web addresses or links
contained in this book may have changed since publication and may no longer be
valid. The views expressed in this work are solely those of the author and do not
necessarily reflect the views of the publisher, and the publisher hereby disclaims any
responsibility for them.

ISBN: 978-1-4401-8887-9 (pbk)
ISBN: 978-1-4401-8888-6 (ebook)

Printed in the United States of America

iUniverse rev. date: 11/6/09

This is dedicated to:

Patrick
Elizabeth
Kellie

Who constantly remind me how effort, appreciation, courtesy, and laughter can co-exist on a daily basis making the world a better place and their father proud.

I

ACKNOWLEDGEMENTS

I wish to acknowledge the people who I wrote about in this book. Their names have been changed but they are real and form the content of true stories.

I also wish to express my gratitude for all of those who feed the hungry and clothe the needy. They are often the same sentient beings who rose above their own adversity by willpower and hard work.

And last but certainly not least I wish to acknowledge the efforts and expertise of Jeannette C. Love, my exemplary administrative assistant, for her hours of review and editing pursuant to this book.

II

PREFACE

Every 26 seconds a vehicle is stolen in the United States. Approximately 1.3 million women and 835,000 men are assaulted by an acquaintance each year. 5.7 million young people are estimated to be involved in bullying in this country. While theses statistics come from federal investigation agencies, federal law figures, and national youth violence centers respectively; there is more information that comes from within our communities. Neighbors are less inclined to help neighbors. In fact, many people don't even know who resides next door to them. People are increasingly exhibiting behaviors that include insult, demand, disrespect, dishonor, fabrication, vile profanity, economic piracy, and physical harm. An increasing number of individuals in our society find it acceptable to violate company rules, municipal regulations, governmental laws, and basic ethical standards. Of course there is also a population of American citizens who extend the hand of fellowship, charity, courtesy, and caring. Unfortunately, the former group is casting a shadow over the latter entity. A common denominator that seems to exist among the aforementioned dysfunctional body is identified with two words – entitlement and delusion.

Books, manuals, and publications exist which describe disease and disorders. A classification by the healthcare industry is given and a number assigned to that particular problem which then classifies it as an official disorder.

The title of this book does not constitute an official disorder. You won't find it in any of those aforementioned books or publications. *Delusional Entitlement Disorder* has not been recognized as a disease by those *powers-that-be* who have the dubious distinction of tapping the disorder on its head with a scepter and bestowing upon it a title of official impairment.

Dr. E. A. Shockney, having spent 37 years in healthcare within the fields of clinical pathology, medical technology, counseling psychology, military medicine, decedent affairs, expert witnessing, behavioral health consulting and forensic psychotherapy; draws from a constellation of histories and experiences in his exploration of this subject.

Pharmaceutical companies have yet to formulate the pill that within twenty minutes of being swallowed reduces the signs and symptoms of *Delusional Entitlement Disorder*.

Radiology researchers haven't developed a multi-gate, super-collimated, gamma-source imaging device that can scan the body and within ten minutes locate the ugly cells from which the *Delusional Entitlement Disorder* originated.

Surgeons haven't been able to perfect the minimally-invasive endoscopic extraction of that terrible *Delusional Entitlement Disorder* mass.

As a general rule, this condition which I term *Delusional-EntitlementDisorder* has not been recognized. Therefore a treatment has not been considered until now. Certainly, the behaviors associated with it are quite visible to the public and are quiet annoying in general. *Delusional Entitlement Disorder* is an attitude. Although it takes on features that make it appear malignant, rapidly spreading, invasive, and contagious; it is still just an attitude that brings about unhealthy behaviors and often subsequent unfavorable results.

Across the nation the court system is realizing an increase in crime and casework that is heavily impacted by adults and youth whose malicious actions are self-serving. Schools are hiring security officers for the purpose of suppressing violence, threats, and bullying. The media seems to project entitlement and self-centeredness in its programming and advertising. Families are increasingly fragmented and divorcing as this book is being written. One must carefully scrutinize negotiations, contracts, and agreements to avoid potential slippery manipulation in the fine print. *Delusional Entitlement Disorder* is present each and every day.

In this book you will be acquainted with *Delusional Entitlement Disorder;* its causes and its impact on communities, societies and families. It is not too late to reverse its progress. Perhaps it will take a generation to do so. I am confident that this pervasive problem can be successfully treated within families. It is a corrective approach that can be started within weeks. Please note however, that this book is not a replacement or substitute for treatment by a licensed healthcare professional. It is an introduction to a problem that exists within our society and a compilation of recommendations pursuant to correcting the problem.

Welcome to the exploration into *Delusional Entitlement Disorder.* Put on your surgical mask, make sure you "glove-up" and pre-operatively "scrub in", and let's go to work.

CONTENTS

— CHAPTER 1 —

INTRODUCTION

As noted in the Preface you will not find *Delusional Entitlement Disorder* in a diagnostic text. However, it makes its presence well known in the attitudes and behaviors of self-absorbed individuals. Furthermore, it is spilling over into families, communities, and business relationships.

What is delusion? In at least one instance it has been defined as *a persistent false belief regarding the self that is maintained despite indisputable evidence to the contrary.*

Then what is entitlement? In a non-legal definition and in a more casual sense *is someone's belief that he or she is deserving of some particular reward or benefit above other individuals.*

When you combine the two terms in the context of this book the individual who possesses these characteristics actually believes that standards, rules, and laws do not apply to them. They believe they are immune from the accountability and expectation to which common people are held.

When does it become a disorder? Disorder is defined as the *opposite of law and order* and/or when *one or more forms of behavior by an individual or group of people creates disturbance or compromises others.*

It this book, I will address **Delusional Entitlement Disorder** (affectionately called **D.E.D.**). It is what I believe is the unofficial disorder that can and is crippling America. Incongruent behaviors by individuals, families, groups and communities based on their false beliefs of superiority are tearing at the priceless fabric of the "pioneer spirit" upon which this great country was founded.

— CHAPTER 2 —

LITTLE JOHNNY

Little Johnny is screaming his head off. He is kicking the seat and banging his fist against the window in the back of the car on the way home as the family leaves the ball field.

Little Johnny did not score the winning goal nor did he receive the ovation he had hoped for from the crowd. He is angry and he is throwing a tantrum. His mother has prepared a home-cooked meal that is waiting for them in the oven. Johnny won't stand for that. He is demanding that he be taken to a local fast-food restaurant. He wants to be rewarded for his bruised ego. He demands to have his favorite meal. He is bellowing insults to his parents, finding fault with his coach, and throwing objects at his sister in the adjacent back seat. He announces that he simply won't tolerate going home for dinner and again demands that they pull into the fast-food facility. And here is where it becomes even more interesting. His parents pull into the fast-food restaurant and enter the drive-through. Johnny does not want to go inside. He wants his food handed to him. Little Johnny is 14 years old.

His parents ask if he is doing okay now that he has his meal. They certainly want him to be comfortable.

The signs and symptoms are classic. Little Johnny:

- *Feels entitled to have what he wants*
- *Has developed the delusional concept that the whole world revolves around him.*

The provisional findings are clear. Little Johnny:

- *Has contracted Delusional Entitlement Disorder*
- *And it looks like D.E.D. has impacted the entire family*

— CHAPTER 3 —

THAT DOESN'T APPLY TO US

As patrons walked into the restaurant they could read the sign that said "**Please Do Not Move the Tables and Chairs.**" A family of four exits their vehicle and enters the eatery. The facility is a very clean and attractive cafe with the seating neatly structured for maximum use and comfort. The father and mother immediately go to a corner of the restaurant and reconfigure the tables and chairs to suit themselves. Their actions cause a couple of tables to be without chairs. Their son, approximately ten-years old, asks his father if he had seen the sign as they entered.

The father replies, "That doesn't apply to us."

Rules, regulations, and standards. It is not uncommon for individuals to feel that certain statutes and parameters do not apply to their personal lives. I have felt that way at times. And there is more than one definition to the phrase *that doesn't apply to us.*

I had the pleasure of taking one of my grandsons on a trip this past year. We passed through the middle states where I showed him many of the sites. While we were down near the Mississippi riverboats, I noticed a sign that said *no skateboarding* near the ramp to the riverboats. I can guarantee that at this point in my life and having never been on a skateboard, that sign didn't apply to me.

On the other hand, the rule did apply my grandson with his energy, willingness, and skateboard agility. This application of the term requires common sense.

The second definition carries with it the characteristics of arrogance and entitlement. The man who required his family to configure the dining area in the restaurant to suit his needs is associated with this toxic definition. His focus was on his comfort despite inconvenience to others. The rule of not moving the tables and chairs along with the request to order food prior to sitting down was structured for courtesy and ease of operation to all the patrons. This individual had no concern for the welfare or courtesy of the other patrons. It was all about *him*. His delusion is that he actually perceives himself to have more importance in the world than others. His entitlement is that he actually believes the eating establishment and its patrons owe him special privilege. The rule was put into force to promote order within the restaurant. What this man did was to create disorder. The action of this man, based on his pattern of rationale and self-ingratiating attitude, created delusion, entitlement, and disorder…the three landmark words associated with this impairment.

But it doesn't stop there. If you recall, the wife was also participating in the disorder alongside her husband. Either she dysfunctionally has the same belief system as her spouse or perhaps his attitude of entitlement has such overbearance that she has simply learned to go along with him in order to avoid causing more chaos. Thus, the wife/mother of the family has also contracted **Delusional Entitlement Disorder** regardless of whether it is direct or indirect in nature.

Remember the son? He brought his father's attention to the sign. He has been placed in a quandary by his father's directives. He will either be taught that

Delusional Entitlement Disorder is appropriate behavior or he will develop resentment to his parents' attitude of special treatment. The latter may result in fragmentation within the family. The former helps develop the young man into another adult with a sense of entitlement.

We often see *D.E.D.* being played out in public venues such as restaurants, grocery lines, and wherever guidelines have been established to minimize the pushing, shoving, and line-crashing that is frequent and repetitive. I have both seen and heard of adults pushing and shoving other adults out of the way when a sale is going on at a department store. The person doing the shoving has the mind-set that they have the right to push others out of the way because they are entitled to claim a sale item at the cost to another patron.

In 1979 a concert took place in Cincinnati where there was open seating. This simply means that the ticket for admission did not guarantee a reserved seat. The seating was *first come-first served.* When the doors to the arena were opened, 11 people were trampled to death and dozens were crushed by those who felt they had the right to claim a preferred seat regardless of the cost to others.

A large number of adults seem to disobey traffic laws, disregard various regulations, and violate legal and ethical standards for a number of reasons. Those reasons almost always incorporate entitlement and the delusion thinking of false sense of superiority. Children develop *Delusional Entitlement Disorder* because they learn it from their parents and grandparents by example.

— CHAPTER 4 —

MOSES

Moses was the newspaper delivery man in a small town of 1,500 residents. He delivered the local newspaper seven days per week for decades. It was said that Moses never missed a delivery. Once he found the proper house the first time, it was virtually guaranteed that your newspaper would be there by 5:00 a.m. every day. Moses was also legally blind. He could see movement but no images.

When a new resident wanted to subscribe to the newspaper, Moses would be summoned. He would find out how many houses from a particular corner was the new subscriber's residence. Once located, he would incorporate that new delivery site to his well-patterned route that he walked each morning.

Moses collected for the newspaper service on Saturday afternoon. He provided each subscriber with a cleanly-washed old baby food jar. He kindly asked that each subscriber pay him in coin since he could determine its denomination with greater ease. Each subscriber was asked to put their coin jar on the corner of their front step each Saturday. Moses would collect the coinage and leave a "paid in full" coupon for the newspaper service in the jar.

Moses and his wife had two children. Moses' spouse was a seamstress who did alterations as well as laundry/ironing for local residents. Moses and his wife Nellie were able to make provisions for both children to attend post-high school education. Moses and Nellie also gave a donation each time there was a need in the community.

Moses delivered the paper to the local parish. The clergy would notice that every ten weeks, Moses would not collect for the paper. He would leave the coins in the old baby food jar. The priest finally asked Moses why he didn't collect on those weeks.

Moses grinned and responded, "Well, the wife reads the Bible to me and it says that we are supposed to give back ten percent to God. So I don't charge the Church every tenth Sunday 'cause it's the right thing to do."

The pastor said to Moses, "I happen to know that you and your wife give a donation to the Church every week. You should charge me for the newspaper."

Moses with his useless squint of both eyes grinned and turned away saying, "It's because it is the right thing to do."

When Moses was found dead one morning from a heart attack on his newspaper delivery route, the community quickly realized what a noble and humble man they had lost. Moses had no earthly idea what delusion was. He was not even remotely acquainted with the term entitlement. However, he knew in his core the definition of stewardship for others and what it meant to *do the right thing.*

I recall discussing the memory of Moses with my parents a few years before their passing. At the conclusion of that conversation, my mother crippled by arthritis left the room to retrieve something. She had kept the old baby food jar that Moses had given them years ago. To them it was a reminder of good people in times past. To me, it represented a token of the antidote *to* **Delusional Entitlement Disorder.**

— CHAPTER 5 —

DARRELL

It was a community social gathering in an area of central Florida where the orange groves peppered the countryside. The attendees ranged from executives who had concluded their careers in the northern part of the country and elected to retire in the south to the workers who actually picked the citrus that grew in the fields.

It was an autumn evening which preceded Thanksgiving by about a week. In the course of the evening the conversations turned mellow as people began reflecting on what they perceived as their blessings in the past year. They chose to share their stories with others.

"I have really been fortunate this year," noted one gentleman, "I bought a couple of small rental properties near here and they have generated enough additional revenue that my wife and I have been able to go on a cruise and vacation in some of the finer spots around the country."

"It was a good year for me too," said another individual with the spouse at his side grinning and nodding, "We bought some stocks from money we inherited from my deceased aunt and that stock went through the roof! We made a killing."

The stories went on for several minutes. At the edge of the group sat a man named Darrell. He was wearing worn but clean workpants and a clean, but faded, t-shirt. He simply sat there grinning. With a majority of the group being aware that Darrell worked as a citrus picker, they wondered what he found amusing.

One of the people asked, "Darrell, why are you grinning? Do you have something on your mind?"

Darrell turned and slowly retorted, "Yes I do, and I guess I got a whole lot to be grateful for."

Of course, this quickly gained the attention of those in attendance.

"Most of you know that my wife died last year and didn't have no life insurance," Darrell said, "and you know that my old truck broke down earlier this year and I couldn't afford to fix it."

The attention of the crowd was fully on Darrell. They were trying to understand his joy. He was a widowed man who picked oranges. He was the father of three children under the age of 10.

"Well you see, when I went to the grocery I had to walk. And since it isn't safe to leave kids alone, I had them walk with me. Well, when I buy four bags of groceries every two weeks, I have to make two trips. Me and the kids have to walk a lot. Well, I found me an old car and the owner was kind enough to let me pay her $50 a month until I get it paid off. So now the kids and me can ride to the grocery, do it in one trip and sometimes we can go to the ice cream place to give ourselves a treat. I would say life is just about perfect for the four of us," said Darrell.

The crowd was speechless. They were in a state of *reality check*. Many had been telling stories of prosperity some of which were on the cusp of indulgence. In this book we speak of entitlement, often arrogance, and frequently the delusion that goes with entitlement. Those characteristics were not present in Darrell's presentation to the group. The exchange with Darrell and his neighbors wasn't about entitlement. It was about perspective and gratitude.

Some at that gathering had based their view of gratitude on financial gain and elegant travel which within itself is certainly reasonable in a hard working society. However, the simplicity and sincerity of Darrell's story and its relationship to his family introduced them to a core value of true thanksgiving.

I am certain that residents who attended the autumn social and heard Darrell's expression of appreciation took special note from that point forward when they saw the old, faded car puttering down the road driven by a man accompanied by three laughing children.

— CHAPTER 6 —

D.E.D. ISN'T ABOUT SOCIOECONOMICS

I have shared the stories of Moses and Darrell with you. You can ascertain that they were not financially wealthy or academically trained. However, I don't want to project that only the poor and uneducated are immune to *D.E.D.* Nor do I wish to suggest that individuals who are successful, wealthy, and hold academic degrees possess *Delusional Entitlement Disorder.*

A sense of entitlement and a pattern of delusional attitude can affect an individual or a family regardless of their economic status, educational achievements, race, culture, gender, occupation, or geographic location. It is the method and attitude by which each and every person approaches life. Blending self-accountability and stewardship for others is a sure pathway to avoid *D.E.D.* When an individual in any demographic focuses on *me first at all cost because I deserve it* they can easily develop into delusional entitlement.

America is filled with stories about people who have originated from meager surroundings who have become very successful in life along side counterparts who were born into luxury. Their success can be measured in many ways including their contribution to family, community, and country. Unfortunately we have also witnessed both the wealthy and less fortunate migrate the other way.

It boils down to combining those opportunities and gifts that we have been given combined with an attitude of appreciation, unselfishness, and charity.

— CHAPTER 7 —

TURNING SLOWLY

Thus far we have explored the stories of Little Johnny, Moses, the family who felt the need to restructure the restaurant for their own comfort, and the adventures of Darrell. It will be rather obvious to you that some of the people in these events strayed from balanced thinking and behavior. Often when things get out of kilter, whether within the self or within society, it seems that getting off course can be a slow and gradual process.

In 1975, I began taking flying lessons. My flight instructor was a retired military officer named John. One day we were flying and he asked me to put on the hood. This is a device much like a welder's mask that fits around the head and restricts the pilot's vision to only the instrument panel. It is used to teach a student pilot how to recognize and utilize the airplane's instruments. Instructor John took the controls for several minutes and had me simply scan the instrument panel. Of course, being new to flight instrumentation, I was not familiar with what I was seeing and what was happening. After about three minutes, John turned and asked me a question.

"Do you think we are in level, straight flight, Ed?" John asked.

My response, "Yep, sure feels like it is, I would have known if we weren't."

John then asked me to lift the hood up which gave me an unrestricted view. When I did, I noticed that things were not where I thought they would be. Where I anticipated sky, there was terra firma. The horizon was sideways We were in a slow turn heading the opposite direction.

After my shock wore off, John laughed for a moment at the look on my face and said, "When you turn slowly and reposition things gradually, a person can be convinced they are headed in one direction when indeed they aren't. In fact they can actually be crashing and not even know it. Changing positions slowly without paying attention can end up with you being horribly off course."

I earned my pilot's license in 1976. I haven't flown small aircraft very much in the past few years. But one factor that has remained firmly in my mind is what John taught me. It is vital to be aware as to what can happen when something turns slowly and a course can be altered.

By the time the person is off course, damage is often present. That is true for aviation. That is equally true for attitude.

I cannot even estimate how many times I have thought of John's illustration over the years as a psychotherapist and used it in the capacity of offering people insight into correcting their health behaviors and attitudes. As we explore *Delusional Entitlement Disorder* in this book, I urge you to keep the *turning slowly* example in mind when figuring out how one get's off balance in mood and action.

— CHAPTER 8 —

NINE MINUTES?

Remember the phrase that states *patience is a virtue*? It certainly applies in several aspects of **D.E.D.**

In the early seventies, I became heavily involved in the unique, highly competitive and brutal sport of boxing. I wasn't a natural, but with approximately 15 hours per week in the gym with trainers and sparring partners coupled with daily running and weight conditioning, I became pretty successful. Shortly after competing in the championship in my division which resulted in my being the runner-up, I took a few months off. I became de-conditioned, started eating less healthy food, ceased jogging, and somewhat abandoned my focused attitude on the sport.

I was fortunate to have two of the most incredible coaches in the boxing business at the time. They weren't fancy nor did they project pompous attitudes. They were real people with sharp pragmatic views of life. John was a police officer who worked with youth. Chris worked with molten metals in a foundry. They were both grounded and realistic.

After slouching for the summer, I returned to the gym that fall. Along with a sparring partner who had been training all summer, I crawled back into the ring for a work-out. I was going to show Coach John and Coach

Chris that I was still the same powerhouse that I had been the previous spring. In my mind, I was right back into the mindset of sparring for three three-minute rounds. In my attitude, I was cocky and brash. In my reality, I was unconditioned, sloppy and had lost a portion of my skill. I had been *turning slowly* during the course of the summer and was off course in many facets.

The result of the time in the ring on that fall evening was disastrous for me. However, I made my sparring partner look very, very good! I had no endurance, I was sloppy in my techniques, my attitude was horrible, and I acted like an idiot. At the conclusion of throwing my gloves, kicking over a stool, and complaining that I didn't know what was going wrong, Coach John approached me.

"So, how long has it been since you trained?" John calmly asked.

"Oh, I don't know… (expletives deleted)...maybe a month or so!" I sputtered and blurted out with a pathetic attitude.

"So let me understand this. You have not worked out in four months, you have stopped following most of the healthy things you were doing, you are stale and way off base, and expect to have everything back to normal in nine minutes?", John asked.

His reference was to the three three-minute rounds of sparring which I was miserably attempting.

In a continuation of my attitude, I threw my equipment against the wall and stomped out. How dare I take this criticism? I am second-ranked in my division!

By the time I arrived home that evening, I had cooled down a bit. I told my father what had happened. He sat there for a moment and then noted, "I think you need to adjust your attitude and apologize to your coaches for the way you acted. Secondly, you were the second-ranked boxer last spring but aren't now. You haven't been working out and have gotten off course. John was right. You can't expect everything you have let go over four months to miraculously come back in nine minutes of working out."

These two individuals had taught me a lesson that stays with me until this day. To keep *on track* an individual has to invest energy and focus on the result they want. And furthermore, a person can't expect improvement overnight. It requires patience, work, and consistency.

The ability to remain in focus and on track requires two elements. The first is an understanding of how a person might have turned slowly and gotten off course. The second is knowing that it will take time, patience, and consistency to get back on track. This needs to be done without a self-centered attitude.

This chapter and the previous one have hopefully enlightened you as to how things can change slowly and not always for the better. They also define how it takes an investment in time and effort to bring things back to where they should be.

These two important factors are significant in approaching **Delusional Entitlement Disorder** as well as other challenges in your life.

— CHAPTER 9 —

I DEMAND MY RIGHTS!

The married father of two storms into the local welfare office. He is enraged that his food subsidy has been interrupted. The screaming and venomous attitude is directed toward the young lady behind the desk. He demands to know why his welfare benefits have been interrupted. He advises the young girl that his rights are being violated. She responds that welfare benefits have been suspended due to his not looking for employment for over six months and his non-completion of the paperwork that is required. She also notes that it has been very frustrating with his rejection of their numerous phone calls to him. The man makes dubious threats and offers several loud insults. As he exit's the office and drives away, the young lady notices that he is driving a new vehicle with the sale bill still affixed to the side window.

In the early writings of India, one of the masters spoke regarding *rights*. The *Bhagavad Gita* describes how the Master told the young prince Arjuna that one has the right to be productive and work but that there was never a right to being rewarded for anything and everything. He further tells him that a person should never engage in action solely for the reward at the end of the effort. There shouldn't be a demand for a reward tied to a person's effort.

I am reminded by a great mentor in my youth as to the difference between a right and a privilege or gift. Trooper Rex, a state policeman of extraordinary character, was a prominent figure in my community in my teenage years. My friends and I, preparing to turn 16, had commented on how we would soon have the *right* to drive. Each time he had the opportunity, Trooper Rex would remind each one of us that we were being given the privilege to drive provided we stay within the law. There was no governmental statute or divine decree that had given us the *right* to operate a motor vehicle. He also reminded us that in order to be offered opportunity and privilege, it required courtesy and respect on our parts toward others in our community.

There is a biblical story about a landowner who hired different workers throughout the day to work in his vineyard. In the twentieth chapter of Matthew, it notes that a landowner hired each worker with a specific understanding of what was expected and a promise to pay that respective worker at the end of their effort. At the conclusion of the workday some of the workers were upset because even though they were paid according to their agreement with the landowner, other workers were paid more. The disgruntled workers in essence demanded their *right* to more pay instead of appreciating the fact that the landowner had rewarded them for their effort as he had agreed. They were envious because of the landowner's generosity to others and it resulted in their demanding their *rights*. Even in ancient times, **Delusional Entitlement Disorder** existed.

Unquestionably, under the laws of government certain rights are given to its citizens. In the examination of the Declaration of Independence and in the

Constitution of the United States, an individual's rights under the law is critical to the nature and structure of those priceless documents and the process by which our forefathers structured the United States of America. But along with rights come rules, standards, responsibility, and expectations as we have mentioned in previous chapters.

As we revisit the irate man in the welfare office, it is easy to recognize that his perception of rights was considerably distorted. Provisions within the local community had been made for those who were disadvantaged through the welfare system. While obvious laws and regulations apply within such agencies, it wasn't those *rights* of which the man was complaining. He felt that he had a *right* to make demands on the welfare office even though he had not complied with what they had asked of him. Additionally, he was demanding financial assistance to take care of his family while at the same time it was apparent he had the resources by which he could purchase a new luxury vehicle. Once again we see the emergence of delusion and entitlement.

— CHAPTER 10 —

ANDY

My initial meeting with Andy involved considerable intimidation. It certainly wasn't me that was the intimidator.

He sat in my office wearing bib-overalls with a t-shirt that permitted his muscularity to be easily visible. With full beard and shoulder-length hair, he greeted me with a very firm handshake yet no visible facial expression other than a wince of pain expressed in his eyes as he arose from the chair.

Andy had sustained injury from his work and he was sent to visit with me regarding his issues of pain and frustration. Upon my inquiring as to the nature of his occupation, he responded that he was a *rod-buster*. Drawing on my limited knowledge of commercial construction, I recalled that a *rod-buster* is the vernacular for an iron worker whose job it was to erect structures such as high-rise buildings, bridges, and assemble large metal objects. This type of work typically requires heavy lifting, welding, and riveting often at considerable heights while walking on a narrow beam during frequent spells of blowing wind and inclement weather.

This mountain man had injured his back doing what he loved. He loved to build things. And it was my job to help him learn how to function more favorably under difficult conditions. As I look back Andy was the one who enlightened me as to the nature of humility, overcoming obstacles, appreciating the nature of the universe, and avoiding entitlement at any cost.

Big Iron Andy as he was nick-named, had served his country as a United States Marine. But his story as an iron worker and Marine didn't stop there. Emerging from a fragmented family, Andy had strove to work hard and provide for his spouse, his daughter, and himself. His goal was to build a safe and happy family unit. Andy's life began to unravel when his wife was diagnosed with a crippling disease. Unable to handle the stress of his wife's disabling health condition, he turned to alcohol in excess and cursed his creator for causing such a mess in his life.

"Why, God...did you let this happen?! What did I ever do to you?! Why did you do this to someone I love?!" Andy later admitted to crying out repeatedly.

Andy's behavior under the influence of alcohol began to cut a wide swath of destruction in his life. His conduct resulted in time spent in jail and required his presence in the court system. He was prevented from driving a motor vehicle and forced into court-mandated substance abuse counseling. His conduct and attitude became angry, belligerent, and self-absorbed.

At some point in his journey, Andy began to realize that it wasn't all about him. He started to develop an understanding that trials and tribulations occur in life and it is what a person does with those challenges that sculpts their purpose in this world. Continuing, he advised that a monumental change began when he started thinking of others, recognizing others who were much worse off than him, and started investing in principles he had learned as a U. S. Marine...honor, service, character and respect.

Soon after this metamorphosis began, he sought personal spiritual strength. Andy rapidly developed an understanding that he was but a small puzzle piece in the structure of the universe. He invested what energy he had remaining in his faith and in God. He soon recognized how many people in the world around him thought of the self as the center of the universe.

Andy began a love affair with something that many individuals take for granted…woodworking. To this day, he can tell you of the marvelous beauty that comes from a tree that originates from a seed, is planted as a sapling and through the divine process of nature, offers warm patterns of texture, shades and color in forms that are designed to protect, provide, and serve mankind. From pieces of wood over the years, Andy has constructed beautiful furniture, household items, and masterpieces. And as he works, he cherishes the origin of the wood and its process of development in nature. While Andy sells most of his masterpieces in order to provide for needs, he also gives many of them away as gifts to those in need.

His transition in life didn't stop at his woodworking. He started giving back to friends, family, and the community. Instead of just thinking about improving his life he actually improved his behaviors in life. If he met someone who had less than he, he would share his resources with them. If someone needed a helping hand, Andy was there to assist. He gained so much insight in his court-mandated counseling that he chose to help others gain control over their problems. Andy began to train as an addiction counselor. At the time of this writing, Big Iron Andy hosts court-related counseling sessions in substance abuse, petty theft, and conduct disorder for teenagers. He suggests in a very powerful manner of presentation of self the principles of honor, service, character, respect, and morality to misdirected young people in his classes. He does so, not with intimidation of his size and strength, but with a soft voice and a direct look into the eyes of the youth.

He will be the first to tell you that his struggles haven't magically evaporated. Andy strives to focus on service and courtesy to others and constant appreciation for the important things in his life in order to avoid falling back into the **D.E.D.** cesspool.

Tragedy struck Andy's life again several months after I had met him. My phone rang one Friday afternoon and it was Andy. His wife's health had continued to deteriorate requiring measurable bed rest and medication. Earlier that afternoon she had decided to take a nap. When Andy went in to check on her, she had passed away in her sleep. His mourning heart was heavy. And even in his mourning, Andy reflected on all the positives his spouse had brought to the world and how grateful he was for her presence in his life.

In the months following the death of his spouse, Andy lost his home, was unable to find employment due to his back injury, and had his charitable nature taken advantage of by manipulative individuals.

Andy maintained his faith, both divinely and in human nature. He thrust his energy into his woodworking and carpentry. He found adaptive ways to work that didn't compromise his chronic pain and limitations. And he does still to this day.

He told me recently that he was working in solitude in his little workshop very early one morning. It was very quiet and peaceful. The sun was rising, birds began chirping, his stomach was full, and he had slept in a warm bed the night before. He noticed how much he was enjoying working with a gorgeous piece of maple and how content he felt. Andy said, "I looked around and realized that my life wasn't so bad, that I had those things I needed in life…not necessarily everything I wanted…felt appreciative of all of my blessings and thought to myself…hmmmm…if I'm not careful I could just end up being happy today."

He ended that story with laughter and a joyful expression on his face.

Big Iron Andy traversed through his own trials, tribulations, and nightmares to discover the formula of not only finding happiness in what is dealt to him every day, but also how to avoid the self-centeredness and toxic thought patterns that define *Delusional Entitlement Disorder.*

Andy had invested his energy into an attitude of gratitude, no matter how small. When you do that, you don't leave much room for self-centered pity, demands of others, nor sense of entitlement.

— CHAPTER 11 —

A DOSE OF PSYCHOEDUCATION

In the beginning of this book, I described how *D.E.D*. was not an official disorder, illness, or impairment. I also noted how you wouldn't find it listed in any number of textbooks or diagnostic manuals. However, it might be most helpful for me to share other *official* disorders with you that may be associated with *D.E.D*. If you want to explore further into these terms, I invite you to research the numerous on-line dictionary references or go to www.psych.org to access publications offering an explanation in more depth.

Here are some definitions for your perusal:

- <u>Disorder:</u>   A lack of order, chaos, confusion, the disturbance of normal function.

- <u>Impairment:</u>   Something that diminishes value, quality or strength.

- <u>Disease:</u>   An abnormal condition that impairs bodily function.

- Ego:

  The self as distinct from the world and other entities. It can also be used to express an exaggerated sense of self, conceit.

- Narcissism

  Excessive love or admiration for one's self.

- Impulse-Control Disorder:

  A condition in which a person has difficulty resisting temptations, drive, or an impulse that can result in harm to self or others.

- Intermittent Explosive Disorder:

  A person's inability to resist aggressive impulses that result in damage.

- Antisocial Behavior:

  Conduct which is not a mental disorder but is characterized by actions that harm and have no regard for others.

- Antisocial Personality:

  This is a pattern of violation of other people and disregard for the rights of others. It is considered a mental disorder. It is a component of the individual's personality.

It is not the intent of this chapter to fully explain terminology and make the reader proficient in the understanding of disorders and illness. It is merely to acquaint you with conditions that often run parallel to what I am defining as ***Delusional Entitlement Disorder***.

— CHAPTER 12 —

PARENTS: YOU NEED TO OBSERVE YOUR CHILD'S SPIRIT AND ATTITUDE

I was in the home of a neighbor a few years ago when they invited me to look at the new light fixture they had installed in their daughter's room. As I finished admiring the wonderful mini-chandelier and turned to walk out of their child's room, a hand-written poem on the wall grabbed my attention. The words that had been written, presumably by their daughter on a piece of paper thumb-tacked to the wall, seared into my brain.

It said, "Life is meant to punish the soul. May I see you in hell. We can be together there so to torment those who need to be crushed."

We finished our visit and I returned to my house. My head was spinning from what I had read. I unsuccessfully attempted to rationalize those words. Perhaps it was a passage from a play or book the child had been asked to memorize at school. Perhaps it was a lyric from some disturbed song. But my mind kept returning to the same premise. What if I had just read a reflection of what the child was experiencing? What if the child were contemplating self-destruction?

I had no choice but to go back and visit with the parents. I told them that I didn't mean to pry into their family but that I had become concerned about something I read on their daughter's wall as they were showing me the lighting fixture. I shared with them that as a result of my profession I pay attention to the behavior of others as a possible indication of problems that may be brewing but not noticed by others.

In response to my informing them of my concern, the mother chuckled and said, "Oh, kids will be kids. I don't pry into my daughter's belongings. It's probably just some silly thing that she heard."

The father was not as passive. His point of concern was not what was affixed to the wall. His conflict was with me.

"Look, I don't nib around in my daughter's room. We were trying to show you a light fixture not get an opinion on our daughter, "he briskly advised.

I graciously apologized for crossing their boundary and politely excused myself. As I left the home, the next statement was even more chilling from the mother, "Oh, no problem, it's no big deal. As I said…kids will be kids."

No big problem? Well perhaps it was indeed a lyric from a depressive song or a passage from a play. Nevertheless, shouldn't a parent first of all observe what is in their child's room? And furthermore, shouldn't writing like that disturb the parent and cause them to want to ask the child?

I lost contact with the family. However, I was pleased to later discover through a mutual friend that the girl was seeing a psychotherapist. My concern was that too many parents turn a blind eye to the spirit and attitude of their children which can be most obvious if the parents simply look at their child's behavior and environment.

What was and is so concerning is that this is another form of **D.E.D.**

The delusion is in the thinking that *my child would never become destructive or emotionally distraught. We give our child everything they need and want.* Therein lies is the entitlement. *They have it good. My child would never cause harm to self or others.* There is the second dose of delusional thought. *I have a lot going on in my own life, kids will be kids.* And again, a second dose of self-centered entitlement.

My profession has transported me into the criminal and juvenile justice system often. I have evaluated or consulted on legal cases involving a large number of individuals, adult and juvenile, charged with crimes. In one particular case, I was asked by an attorney to assess a 16 year old boy who had been charged with a crime.

When I met with this young man I was amazed at his brief but frightening criminal history as well as his belligerent attitude. To summarize, he had been involved in 4 events of criminal activity including assault and car theft prior to the age of 16.

I was asked by the family's attorney to join him in the conference with the young man and his parents.

One of the parents' started the briefing by stating, "This isn't fair. Joey is such a good boy."

The attorney, a seasoned and well-reputed veteran of the court system, looked at the parents and said, "I beg to differ, and Joey was a good little boy perhaps when he was 5 or 6. Your son has a serious long-term problem and is facing multiple charges that the police can indeed prove. And please keep in mind that Joey left several victims in his wake."

The attorney went on with his discussion with the parents. The erosion of Joey's behavior did not occur overnight. His conduct did not suddenly plummet, but deteriorated over several years. The signs were there all along. Joey lacked structure, sought the easy way to do anything and everything, and assumed less and less responsibility. The attorney aptly noted that this young man had most likely been exhibiting disturbing behavior for several years which would have served as warning signs. But the parents had elected to avoid watching and addressing the behavior and attitude of their child. Again, within that formula lays delusion and entitlement.

"Did the two of you not see the changes in Joey over the past few years?" the attorney asked.

"Listen, we have our own lives to live." the father tersely replied, "We don't have time to watch every little thing our kid does."

"I suggest that all of us as parents should be in touch with our children's actions, likes, dislikes, motivations, fears, assets, and faults," the irritated attorney continued, "It is my responsibility as a parent and your responsibility as parents. Perhaps if we all did that, we could reduce the problems our children have."

And what was the parents' response? They abruptly fired the lawyer and exited the room.

Parents as you will read at another point in this book, it is allowable to inspect your child's room and it is vital that you look around to see what attitudes, behaviors, and attachments your child might possess. Your child indeed is permitted privacy. And they are also offered an opportunity to be well connected to the family through conversation and participation.

D.E.D. in these scenarios points to the delusion that [a] everything is all right and my child would never get involved in harmful things and [b] our family is above and beyond harmful juvenile attitudes and behavior. Also, **D.E.D.** identifies within this setting that the entitlement may rest in the thoughts that [a] if I provide materially for my child, I don't need to be bothered with their attitude, [b] I have my own life and I shouldn't be bothered with my child's silly attitude.

Please spend time with your children and invest energy in observing the things in their life that are a reflection of who they are and what they may be becoming. This is reality. That is responsibility.

In the past ten years, our nation has been plagued with episodes of violence, self-harm, and tragedy to others that has originated from disturbed youth. As authorities have examined the homes of these young people, it has been made known that numerous tell-tale signs were present. In many cases, tragedy and death could have been avoided if only the other family members would have observed more closely.

If you do just that, it increases the possibility that you might avoid tragedy in the family while instilling parental participation that can positively direct generations in your family to come.

If you invest in knowing your children and them understanding you it will offer you an opportunity to not only avoid *D.E.D.*, but also form a healthy and happy family nucleus from which the structure of our society is built.

— CHAPTER 13 —

POTATOES AND OTHER STUFF

The lady shopping at the grocery stopped and looked at a product in the frozen food section. She smiled and shook her head. She recalled the many potatoes she had peeled in the years prior to the advent of instant mashed potato flakes. She reflected on the hundreds of meals she had prepared for her children, now grown. She thought how she and her husband had taught their children to be self-sufficient and not always look for the easy way to do something.

The lady looked again at the container of *microwaveable, pre-cooked, pre-whipped and pre-buttered mashed potatoes* laughed and walked away.

I heard it said many years ago, "We as a nation have become so over-developed that we have become underdeveloped".

We have exercise machines that can be attached to the body which invoke electrical stimulation to the muscles. The machines are designed to stimulate and flex the muscles in order to get development without exercise. It is designed in a manner that permits the user to sit and watch television while the machine works out their muscles.

We have vacuum cleaners that can roam throughout the house independently sweeping the carpets and floors without an operator.

A man pauses and looks down at his shoes. They are scuffed and drab. As a result, he purchased a new pair of shoes. Perhaps he hasn't heard of shoe polish, doesn't know how to operate such a product, or perhaps he considers it beneath him to do so.

The floor and furniture in the young woman's room is laden with clothes. When she removes an article of clothing it is simply flung over something. Her clothes have been walked on, crushed, or remained in a crumpled ball in the corner of the room for days or weeks. When she tries to brush them off and wear them, her clothing is in shambles. Her rationale is that it is time for new clothing anyway. No big deal. Perhaps in her perceived world clothes hangers, closets, laundering/dry cleaning, and ironing is beneath her. It is easier to buy new clothes.

Inventions and technological advances are indeed wonderful. However, without our maintaining perspective and gratitude we as a society have a propensity to take for granted the ultra-modern innovations of today. And we aren't careful, we become exceedingly lazy.

Indeed, in many ways we as a nation have become so overdeveloped that we are truly underdeveloped.

— CHAPTER 14 —

EIGHT WAYS TO GROW

The human race has been seeking a quest for balance and happiness throughout its entire existence. Many theories have surfaced and man just keeps on searching. Several centuries ago and in search for the key to peace and happiness, a mindful philosophy was born that has survived time, trials, and tribulations. It is still used today by many people throughout the world. It is termed the *Eightfold Path.*

This philosophy is based on eight pathways designed to reduce or end mankind's perception of suffering. We are asked to examine the manner by which we look at things that confront us, be able to identify our intentions before taking action, it is suggested that we ensure our speech and the way we talk to others is balanced, it is good for us to direct ourselves to ensure that the actions we take are not malicious, and it is recommended that we seek a livelihood that isn't destructive to society. The Eightfold Path also exhorts us to give the appropriate degree of effort, it asks that we maintain mindfulness in the things that we do throughout the day, and suggests that we invest the right amount of concentration on our effort and actions. Let's take a moment and explore each of those values individually.

How Do I View Things?

When a situation arises in my life, do I look at the problem objectively? Do I stand back and examine it from several points of view? Or do I set my thoughts on the way I want the results to turn out in a manner that favors me? Do I look at the situation from an ethical and moral view within my own values of ethics and morality? Do I examine how my actions may impact or harm myself or others? Or do I perceive the problem from the perspective of how everyone can benefit me? A person cannot tilt their head to one side and expect to attain a level view of what they are looking at. Likewise, we must view a problem or situation as balanced as possible in order to make healthy decisions.

What Is My Intent?

Prior to taking action, forming a plan, or offering advice, the healthy individual should explore his or her intention. Only each individual knows his or her own true intent before putting thoughts or feelings into action. All of us have made choices and engaged in behavior that may not have worked out in the manner we thought it would. That is simply the rhythm of life. Situations don't always work out the way we planned. However, if we enter into attitude or behavior with harmful intent, it certainly makes the environment in which we and the other people live more toxic. Often times, people don't stop and reflect inwardly as to the actual intent they have. To create a more balanced and less toxic world with minimal *D.E.D.*, it is vital to explore our intention before we take action. We should identify our intention before writing the letter, making the phone call, offering a statement, or engaging in a particular behavior. Is it in the best interest of all involved or is in intended to cause someone harm?

Have I Taken The Time To Examine What I Am About To Say?

Speaking correctly is a vital component of forming a less abrasive world and developing less tumultuous relationships. It is also an excellent pathway to reducing **D.E.D.** The words that come out of our mouths can be more painful and destructive than physical assault. Harsh language is very harmful and can produce sizeable scars. We should explore the verbal methods by which we convey our thoughts and emotions in a less harsh manner yet get our point across. Gossip is rampant in today's society and has caused more pain, damage, distorted problems, and ruined more people than we can imagine. Slanderous remarks serve no healthy purpose. Either the statement is valid or it should not be verbalized. Idle chatter, talking for the sake of talking, is useless. How many of us have known someone who talks for the purpose of gaining attention and hearing themselves talk? It is a frequent event in our society. I have caught myself talking without purpose on many occasions. If what you are about to say has no purpose, you probably should not say it. All of us have fallen prey to the problem of unproductive and toxic talk. To improve your life and to reduce **D.E.D.** you should strive to do the following. Ask yourself if what you are about to say is true. Ask yourself if what you are about to say has purpose and is valid. Are you talking just to be talking? Are you spreading gossip or misconstruing something that you don't know to be valid? Correcting the patterns of *right speech* can remedy problems before they start, can cultivate a healthier personal environment, and avoid *Delusional Entitlement Disorder*.

What Will Be The Impact of My Actions?

A very profound theory regarding the actions we take can be found in eastern philosophies as well as a therapeutic method called *Task-Enhanced Therapy*SM. With regard to that particular subject, it has been established that emotions are generally spontaneous events that can't be immediately controlled. We just experience them. Likewise, our thought process is something that is generated within the mind over which we have very little ability to spontaneously alter. Our thoughts are a product of our intellectual process coupled with life experiences. When we experience emotions and thoughts; we should acknowledge them, determine what it is we can learn from them, strive to avoid investing in unnecessary time on non-productive emotions/thoughts, and appreciate wholesome emotions/thoughts. The element over which we have the most control are our actions. Except for those with issues of mental impairment, we as humans are held accountable for our behavioral choices. Our behaviors are also our actions. How much better the world would be if all people would take a few seconds and ask themselves, "What will be the result of my actions and what effect will it have on others?" Harmful actions, much like harsh words, are impossible to reverse once they are released. It is often that we realize that harm, hatred, injury, violence, and conflict could have been completely avoided had the individual explored the impact of their actions prior to engaging them.

Does My Livelihood, My Profession, My Work Contribute To Society or Compromise It?

The reasons why people select careers or occupations are many. Perhaps they are attracted to a particular type of work. Maybe they have skills in which they excel in a specific area. Often, individuals seek a livelihood based on the income they can achieve from a particular type of work. There are those who are drawn to a type of work that offers them control and power. As noted, the reasons are many. In this book we are obviously examining how behaviors and choices support or oppose the unofficial *Delusional Entitlement Disorder*. This plays into our reflection on career and employment. The question to ask one's self is "Does my work contribute to society or compromise the integrity of society?" Please keep in mind that occupations exist in which some people's lives are made better by your work and others may suffer because of your work. We see that in a variety of positions of employment. Thus, people can be helped and possibly harmed at the same time. You must ask the question as it pertains to society: "Does my livelihood contribute to society or compromise it overall?"

Contributors to society rarely contract *D.E.D*. Compromisers to society not only have *D.E.D.,* but they are usually miserable in their work regardless of the money or power they accumulate.

Do I Invest The Right Effort in What I Do?

There are those who do just enough to *get by*. There are those who go the extra mile in completing the task and helping their fellow man. Another population tries to do *not too much* and *not too little*. They simply gauge themselves in the middle to be safe. A fourth group has no intention of investing any effort whatsoever. While two of the first groups have **D.E.D**. in some form, the last group is drenched with full blown *delusional entitlement.* The healthy individual always seeks to invest the right degree of effort in whatever they do from weeding in the garden to serving soup at the local food pantry for the underprivileged.

Do We Keep Our Mind On What We Are Doing?

Several years ago, a retired judge friend asked me if I knew what the most important thing in the world should be to us at that moment. After figuratively scratching my head for a moment, I responded that it must be world peace, discovery for the cure to cancer, or something of great global importance. He smiled at me and replied that the key to his question in a re-phrased form was "what should be important to **us** at the moment". He continued by saying that the most important thing going on at that moment in *our worlds* was the conversation between the two of us because it was the only real thing going on in our lives. It took me a few minutes and some further thoughts from him to understand that we need to pay attention to the event in which we are currently involved. We can't change what has occurred in the past nor can we spontaneously alter the future. We also can't have direct impact on those events in the world, regardless of how globally important they are. We should be "mindful" about current events in which we are presently engaged. We have greater potential for making that moment more impacting and positive. Individuals with **D.E.D.** often do not maintain attention on what they are doing at the moment because they are always daydreaming as to what the world can do for them or what the universe owes them. When we maintain mindfulness on the task we are doing, we do it better, we appreciate more of the things associated with the task, and we sense a feeling of accomplishment when the deed is done.

Do We Maintain Concentration on What We are Doing?

Concentration is not far removed from the previous section that pertained to mindfulness. When we speak of concentration on what we are doing, we are suggesting that we keep all our senses in tune with the task. Are we listening, viewing, touching, and sensing, feeling, and understanding all that is going on as we do our task? If we do, we become much better at what we do. If we permit our minds and attention to scatter to everything from daydreaming to jealousy of others to methods by which we can manipulate others; we not only cultivate features of **D.E.D.,** we also become unhappy and often result to blaming others for our misfortune.

Adopting the improved focus of these eight factors does not occur over night. It is a slow gradual process of which we need to be aware. Integrating some or all of these factors into our daily agenda directs us toward being more of a contribution to society, family and community. The non-use of some or all of these factors brings us closer to being *diagnosed* with **Delusional Entitlement Disorder.**

— CHAPTER 15 —

CHILD TO PARENT D.E.D.

The scenario is something like this. A lady is sitting in her living room listening to the neighbor who has just been informed that she has a serious illness. As the lady offers support to the neighbor, the telephone begins to ring. Knowing that the call will go to the answering machine and determining that her bereaved neighbor's needs are more significant, she elects to not answer the phone. Within less than thirty seconds, her cell phone next to her begins to ring. Again, she realizes that the neighbor's struggle with a potentially fatal illness takes priority. Within a minute, her cell phone starts ringing repeatedly. Someone is incessantly redialing her.

She interrupts the neighbor in order to answer the persistent cell phone. The exchange goes something like this.

<u>Child In Late Teens:</u>	"Mom! Why didn't you answer me when I called?! What is your problem?!"
<u>Parent:</u>	"Well honey, I was busy talking to Mrs. Smith next door. She had something that is very important she needed to discuss with me."

<u>Teenager:</u>	"Oh yeah, I get it. The neighbor is more important than your daughter! Gosh Mom, get with it! (Expletive) I called the house then I had to call your cell three times to get you to pick up!"
<u>Parent:</u>	"Oh, I am so sorry honey, I should have looked at the phone and saw it was you calling. I am so sorry."
<u>Teenager:</u>	"Yeah well....oh wait a minute...I have another call...hang on...I will be right back."

(Parent is on hold in her living room while the overwhelmed Mrs. Smith sits quietly...the daughter comes back on the phone in about 2 minutes)

<u>Teenager:</u>	"Okay Mom, that was my best friend...I had to take the call.... so Mom I need you to go to the store and pick me up some pale red lip gloss...I will need it for tonight."
<u>Parent:</u>	"Well honey, I hadn't planned on going to the store this afternoon. I am sitting her with Mrs. Smith and we need to talk for a while."
<u>Teenager:</u>	"What?! Well, I need you to go to the store anyway because I gotta have that gloss for tonight!?"

<u>Parent:</u>	"What's tonight? Are you going somewhere?"
<u>Teenager:</u>	"Geez Mom! Get with it! Don't you remember anything? What is your problem? I told you a thousand times that I am going to Ginny's party and you forgot?! Geez…what is that about?!" *(sarcastic laugh)*
<u>Parent:</u>	"Oh, I am so sorry honey. I must have forgotten. Well, how about you stop on the way home and get the gloss, I am kind of busy."
<u>Teenager:</u>	"Mom!! What is with you!? I have to go to the tanning salon, I don't have time to go to the store! Tell Mrs. Smith you will talk to her later! Go pick up the gloss for me okay? I will love you forever if you do!"

Sadly, the parent actually tells her neighbor that she has an errand to run, terminates their conversation about Mrs. Smith's illness, and asks if they can get together for tea later. Of course, it certainly appears from the scenario that Mrs. Smith doesn't need tea later. She needs a friend in whom she can confide now.

The story doesn't stop there. When the daughter arrives home shortly before dinner time, she does not thank her mother for getting the lip gloss. But she certainly complains to mother and father who have waited to have dinner with her that she finds the meal that has been prepared as disgusting.

There are several maladaptive factors that rapidly rise to the surface when one reads this scenario.

The factors that emerge in this story include:

- *The delusional attitude of demand by the daughter*
- *The self-centered sense of entitlement held by the daughter*
- *The apologetic delusion by the mother*
- *The apparent unwillingness to hold the teenager to a standard of acceptable conduct and attitude*
- *Emotional blackmail by the daughter*

The first four maladaptive features of this scenario meet the criteria for *Delusional Entitlement Disorder*. The first two demonstrate the pervasive *D.E.D.* that has infected the daughter and is obviously a behavioral choice with which she feels very comfortable. Demand, entitlement, and disrespect. The second two factors illustrate how the parent is actually permitting the teenager to believe that she (the daughter) is the center of the world and that all events should respond to the daughter.

The last dysfunctional factor is equally disturbing. Remember when the daughter told the mother that if she bought the lip gloss for her that the daughter would love her mother forever? Not only does that imply, both consciously and subconsciously that the daughter will refuse to love her mother forever if she doesn't do as she is asked it also sends the signal that children in this family use the tactic of emotional blackmail frequently and with ease.

Should we tie the daughter to the whipping post and flog her? Not so quickly. Let's slow this down and look more closely. The daughter's attitude and behavior is not something that suddenly emerged on the scene.

Dr. Cecil Deckard, a family physician with whom I had the pleasure of working several years ago, told me about an incident during his years in medical school. He recounted how he was put on the spot by one his professors. He was asked to define some particular syndrome. As he was trying to explain what he knew about the particular disorder, the professor was chiding and brow-beating him as to why he wasn't answering to the professor's expectation. Then medical-student Deckard responded to the professor that he was responding to the best of his ability and he was *simply the product of what he had been taught.*

As Dr. Deckard later stated, his remark could have been the end of his medical education but instead his comment was respectfully received by the professor as being valid.

As is typically the case, the person who is displaying behavioral and attitude found to be unacceptable is merely demonstrating what they have seen, been taught or what has been tolerated within their environment.

Let's go back to the girl on the phone with her mother. The teenager in the scenario was indeed exhibiting the peculiar thinking and even more obnoxious conduct that fits the description of **Delusional Entitlement Disorder.** However, it is something that she learned from others and which had not been appropriately addressed by the authority figures in her life…her parent or parents.

Respect, conduct, manners, and proper attitude is something that should be present even before the child is born. A child that is raised with an understanding of gratitude, appreciation, respect for others, a concept of sharing, and a foundation built on compassion is highly likely to avoid contracting the ugly *Delusional Entitlement Disorder.*

By the time a person reaches the age of 17, it is too late to begin teaching those principles. The parents should have started 18 years earlier.

— CHAPTER 16 —

HURRY UP...I AM LATE FOR WORK!

On my way to the office, I had an urge for a cup of hot chai tea. As I sat in the drive-through lane at the local coffee establishment, I experienced an event that simply had to be included in this book.

As the cars slowly negotiated the serpentine driveway picking up their beverages, a car horn started blaring from two or three vehicles behind me. The woman driving the vehicle was making obvious facial gestures that I could see in my rear-view mirror as she honked. I could also see the confused and partially perplexed look on the faces of the other patrons as we slowly progressed in the drive-through. And then it happened.

The woman rolled down her window and shouted, "Hurry up...up there... I am late for work!"

My astonishment had not yet worn off when she shouted again, "Get it moving up there...you are going to make me late!"

As a result of her second bellowing, my now dysfunctional impulse-control system was urging me to offer her some poignant advice in very crisp vernacular that I had learned as a sailor. But I quickly restrained myself understanding that my bellowing back to her was just as obnoxious as her behavior. So I took a few minutes to ask myself what I had just learned from this other driver.

The poor dear was suffering from **D.E.D.** Perhaps she had not planned accordingly that morning and given herself adequate time to both stop by the coffee shop and make it to work on time. Perhaps she had some conflict at home that morning disrupting her normal routine. It was also possible that there were more cars in the beverage drive-through than she had anticipated. All of those possibilities are plausible, but that wasn't the point. The irate driver was trying to hold others responsible for her poor planning and her unreasonable expectations. The two characteristics that form that faulty foundation are [a] her level of entitlement and [b] her delusional thinking.

- *How dare the cars in front of her and the person waiting on the customers not understand she needs to be to work on time*
- *Don't they understand the need for them to adjust their agenda to facilitate her needs?*
- *Can't they get it through their heads that her cup of coffee is more important than the requests of the other patrons?*
- *And do they realize that the reason she will give her boss for being late is due to those stupid people at the coffee shop?*

Realistically, all of us have done the same thing at one time or another. A few months ago as I was driving, an important call rang into my cell phone. I pulled over in order to write down the information. At first I couldn't find a piece of paper on which to write.

For a brief moment I thought to myself, "Why can't this guy wait until I get to the office where I can more easily write this down?" *(The reality check is that I had actually asked this person to call my cell phone at any time.)*

My second episode of **D.E.D.** in that given experience was when the pen with which I was attempting to write didn't work.

"Who gave me this stupid pen? Why doesn't this stupid thing work? People shouldn't make junk like this!"

Great. Now I am talking to an ink pen blaming it for its lack of intelligence and poor work ethic.

How often it is that people blame others for the inability to plan accordingly on their own behalf. Instead of slowing down the process and making adjustments, we have a tendency to vent to anyone or anything we opine should assume responsibility for us. That *reeks* of both entitlement and faulty thinking.

A spiritual leader once said, *"We have a tendency to feel like life is passing us by, so we try to speed up and cram more into a smaller portion of time. This creates friction, frustration, anger, disappointment and often results in our blaming others. If a person plans accordingly, slows down their hectic agenda, participates in those things that are important, cast aside those activities that serve no purpose we actually slow down the pace of life and live it more fully and in an awakened state."*

Thus, the lesson appears to be to assume more responsibility for better planning, blame others less, try to be efficient but not overload one's self to the point of chaos, and to savor our daily experiences instead of viewing them as a personal attack.

— CHAPTER 17 —

GREED, HATRED AND IGNORANCE

I had the opportunity to visit with a man who said he had always experienced difficulty in being able to "wrap his mind" around how to properly treat other people when he was under stress. He stated that he believes he has a kind attitude but when he gets embroiled in the throes of chaos, frustration and worry, his ability to be compassionate to others takes a side street to his primary neurotic concern of taking care of himself. In his years of trying to conquer this problem he studied the works of many masters of mindfulness and behavior. No matter how hard he tried, when faced with conflict and chaos, any skill he had developed that was designed to be compassionate to his fellow man seemed to fail.

He said that he finally learned a simple method that has been around for centuries. It required him to only prevent three things: *greed, hatred and ignorance.* He tried to reduce his complex problem to those three elements. And it worked! He didn't need to have an elaborate plan. He simply had to avoid being greedy, feeling and acting on hatred, and being willing to learn more about the world he lived in and the people with whom he shared that same world.

When we examine greed, we find it may come in many forms. It could be jealousy, seeking to control others, and being self-serving among other things. For this gentleman, all he had to do was when facing a challenge, conflict or decision was ask himself "Am I being greedy about this?"

The same went for his level of disgust, distaste, or hatred for people or events that came into his life. He wondered how many times when confronted with something that he opposed or with which he felt incompatible, he had muttered, "*I just hate that.*" Upon recognizing the thought or verbal utterance of hate, he could recognize the need to change the manner in which he was approaching the problem. He understood that everyone experiences events that frustrate or irritate them. They may encounter things in life that disgust them. Those are feelings that rise naturally in human beings that take time to restructure. But the feeling and presence of hatred is something this gentleman decided needed to be stricken from his mental and verbal vocabulary. He found that once he stopped using the term verbally, he seemed to think it less. Over time, his response to those things he found distasteful began to register in his emotions and thoughts in the terms of something he didn't prefer and chose to avoid instead of things he hated.

And finally, he approached ignorance the same way. The gentleman discovered that the more time he invested in learning or asking about something that was foreign to him, the less uneasy or threatened he felt by the unknown. He would spend energy in discussion, reading, or inquiring about elements in life of which he knew very little but was curious. He didn't always agree with whatever it was. But at least he knew more about it and thus, in most cases, felt less threatened by it. Over the course of time, this man realized that ignorance is not stupidity but merely *not knowing*. Instead of shutting his mind and forming the opinion that something was useless, wrong, or stupid; he expanded his knowledge and then formed an opinion as to whether it was something that he would engrain in his life, personal ethics, and personal moral values.

He had found a structure that helped him deal more favorably with life's experiences. He avoided greed, hatred, and ignorance. And as he did, he reduced his exposure to delusion, arrogance, and any sense of entitlement.

— CHAPTER 18 —

PIONEER ATTITUDE

They traveled in horse-drawn wagons, some covered and some with full exposure to the elements. Pioneers pulled handcarts with their meager belongings aboard along with perhaps a spouse and small children. The offspring, who could walk, trekked alongside the wagon train which was comprised of early settlers forging their way across the early and primitive United States in search of a place where they could settle their families and construct a basic home for shelter.

When a member of one of the pioneer families died enroute, the wagon train would stop for a short while to bury their dead alongside the trail in a makeshift grave then move on. Their perceived extravagances were cool water, new hides and fabric for clothing, fresh vegetables, sunshine, and healthy animals to help them till the land as well as for transportation.

A generation or two later, the pioneer spirit was kept alive by Americans who literally fought for their freedom from adversaries at home and abroad. They did not take for granted the freedom, property, and privileges with which they had been blessed. As automation and machinery had developed by this time, a family typically owned one car and did everything they could to keep it well maintained and serviced. By taking care of what they owned, their automobile was often kept in use for about a decade. To own a home was a great achievement. Pride and respect for those items owned was seen in the form of well-maintained and groomed property.

Neighbors knew each other. They watched over each other's properties, families, and well-being. Up through the 1950's and 1960's, if a community resident was ill or had been impacted by tragedy, the neighbors stepped forward with physical reinforcement, nourishment, financial resources, and moral support. I can easily remember my family, both immediate and extended, taking meals and supplies to neighbors in need. I recall neighbors offering to transport another ailing resident to a doctor's appointment or to the store. Within my own immediate family, it is well within my memory the many times we took clothing that we had outgrown to shelters for the needy instead of discarding them.

Within the past couple of generations, we have observed some once deemed vital occupations go by the wayside. Shoe cobblers would repair footwear. Seamstresses would alter clothing. Appliance repair personnel could fix household fixtures that sustained our everyday existence. Many additional professions were designed to repair and preserve those items we owned in order to keep them in working order. In this day and age, it is more convenient to discard instead of repair. How often it is that people simply buy a new item, appliance, or apparel instead of maintaining or repairing it. I am saddened by the gradual disappearance of many of the old trades and crafts.

Healthcare and health maintenance has changed as well. Only a generation or two past, families knew how to treat minor injuries, colds/flu, and minor digestive disorders. Less and less homes own basic health supplies or even first-aid materials. Their philosophy is that it is easier to take the minor injury or illness to the clinic, emergency room, or physician. Likewise it is more convenient to charge simple care to their insurance, credit card or welfare fund than take the time and effort to stabilize the minor problem at home.

In past generations, adults were willing to literally give their lives for their children. In current times, we see parents putting themselves in higher priority than the children they brought into this world. In more horrible and tragic terms, we actually have seen some adults sacrificing the lives of their own children and spouses in order to satisfy their own wants, desires, addictions, and greed.

The pioneers of this great country would travel thousands of miles through treacherous country to whittle out a meager existence for their family. Now we have individuals who won't cross the street to help a neighbor in need.

What has happened? Too many people in this great country have been infected with greed, self-centeredness, a sense of entitlement, and at attitude that they are "owed". It is the unofficial, but dreaded disease, ***Delusional Entitlement Disorder.***

— CHAPTER 19 —

THE THREE-LEGGED STOOL

Have you ever seen a *three-legged stool*? In years past, we called it a three-legged milking stool as a result of their common presence in dairy barns. The legs were configured in a triangular pattern with weight distributed equally among them.

The use of a three-legged stool as an analogy is quite effective when demonstrating interdependence.

An individual, even though they may possess great agility and coordination, will experience difficulty keeping the little stool upright if balancing on one or two of the legs.

In this book, I use the three-legged stool example to offer a resolution to conflict in today's self-centered society. In subsequent chapters you will read about charity, unity, and fraternity. Imagine each characteristic as a leg on the stool of which we spoke. It will create an image in your mind and a lesson in your consciousness.

— CHAPTER 20 —

WHAT IS CHARITY?

The word *charity* has several definitions. It can mean assisting the poor, giving something to those who are needy, or extending a helping hand to someone less fortunate than you. It can also apply to donating time, belongings, or talent in the spirit of generosity toward humanity.

I would like to suggest that there is at least one more important definition to the term charity. It has been said that charity can be defined as restraining one's self when one has the urge to judge others.

Regardless of how you specifically define charity, the spirit of this great characteristic is one of the three factors by which *Delusional Entitlement Disorder* can be essentially quashed. I recall stories from youth which served as lessons in charity.

One afternoon a neighbor came to our house in a highly frustrated state. She was upset after having taken a casserole to another neighbor who had a family member injured in a serious accident. My mother inquired as to the nature of her frustration.

She responded, "You know I spent quite a bit of time preparing that dish. They didn't invite me in, all I got was a quick thank you, and they didn't tell me anything about the accident. I sure didn't appreciate being treated like that!"

My father, sitting in the other room reading the newspaper, had a puzzled look on his face. He turned to our neighbor calling her by her first name and said, "You know the meaning of charity is when you give something with no intention of getting anything in return."

She spun on her heels and as she went out our door retorted, "Well, I expected to be appreciated a bit more than I was!"

I was a student in Mrs. Smith's second grade class. It was nearing the Christmas holiday and we had been told that there would be a gift exchange between students on the last day of school before vacation. One of the rules to our gift exchange was that you couldn't receive a gift if you didn't bring one for someone else.

Charlie was my classmate. Even though I couldn't comprehend it at the time, Charlie was the poorest kid I knew. Even on the coldest days, he would come to school with no coat and a t-shirt he had outgrown. Shortly after the gift exchange was announced, Charlie approached the teacher's desk.

"I can't bring no gift…we got no money," he told the teacher.

The teacher didn't seem to have much understanding of the problems within Charlie's family. She reiterated that he had to bring a gift of some nature in order to receive one. I was deeply bothered by Charlie's dilemma.

I told my parents at dinner that evening what I had experienced. My father listened and then said, "Don't worry about it, these things have ways of working themselves out."

Dad's statement bothered me. It seemed very unkind.

A couple of nights later, I accompanied my parents to the department store. With my parents' help I purchased a small globe of the earth to give as my present.

The school Christmas party and gift exchange occurred a few days later. A girl in my class was the recipient of the globe I had purchased. The gift I received was a long mural upon which I could paint. I looked over at Charlie and he was laughing and smiling. By some miracle, Charlie had a gift to submit and one to receive!

I arrived home that afternoon and announced to my parents what had happened to Charlie. They said nothing but simply smiled.

Many years and holidays have come and gone. I had periodically thought about Charlie and his gift. It finally struck me that wrapping paper of my gift, the gift Charlie received, the gift that was given in Charlie's name was the same.

A few years before their passing, I asked my parents about Charlie's gift and asked them if they remembered the story. They both gave the same smile that I remembered back at the time of the situation. For several years a group of parents had gone to the local elementary school and met with various teachers ensuring that the underprivileged children received something for the Holidays. Their efforts didn't invoke public recognition or require expectation in return. Those parents, mine included, were simply offering an act of charity.

Charity can be considered contagious. When an individual or family is helped by the charitable actions of others, it commonly sets into motion a sense of wanting to offer charity to others by the person or persons that were themselves helped.

— CHAPTER 21 —

PLACING UNITY IN YOUR LIFE

The charioteer for a great warrior looked down on a valley where two armies were facing one another. Two conflicting groups within a family had fostered so much conflict that they were ready to war against each other. From their individual families, wealth, and those who were in servitude to them; they had both built armies. This wasn't a clash between two countries or two cultures. This was about to be an armed conflict between warring factions of the same family. The charioteer turned to the prince for whom he drove and asked his thoughts.

"Though they are overpowered by greed and see no evil in destroying families or injuring friends, we see these as evils," the prince proclaimed, "where there is no sense of unity, the members of the family become corrupt; and with the corruption of the people, society is plunged into chaos. When chaos thrives it becomes hell. It disrupts the process of spiritual evolution within the people, destroys the foundations of family and society and violates the unity of life."

My Uncle Howard raised Belgian draft horses. I can recall as a child the size of one of those working creatures. I also recall that while the strength of one horse was impressive what could be done when several of the horses were harnessed as a team was amazing. The strength and power of a team of horses often appears unstoppable. When a team of horses work together they seem to be able to not only support the equine that may be weaker than the others but there is also a spirit of camaraderie that is formed that encourages all of the horses to pull together in greater force. This is a definition of unity.

What are some of the forces of unity to which we can harness together and form an arsenal of goodness? They include:

- *Our immediate family*
- *Our extended family*
- *Our neighborhood*
- *Our community*
- *School groups and clubs*
- *Church, spiritual or religious affiliations*
- *Charities*
- *Community service groups*

People congregate to worship or study and when they do it is not uncommon to feel the quantum of energy that is formed from that unity. In Eastern philosophy and culture, a *sangha* is where several people come together to meditate, study and work toward a goal of unity. In Western religious culture it is called a congregation or a parish.

I encourage each one of you to examine your sources of unity and strength. Not just because there is strength in numbers but also because in unified groups where a positive sense of harmony and productive strength exists there is less chance for a sense of entitlement and delusional view of life.

If you don't think that there is a thirst for belonging and unity, look around you at the gang culture that is prolific in the societies throughout the world. Individuals become affiliated with gangs for the purpose of unity, a sense of belonging and an attachment to something that is familial.

Strengthen your unity not just within your family but also within your community. By working in harmony and functioning together, so much more can be achieved.

Whether it be your immediate family, your extended family, those residents on your block or near your farm, the people in your neighborhood or community, your fellow members of a parish, sangha or congregation, or the other parents in your child's school; strive for unity and watch the energy of positive power transform the world to a better place.

— CHAPTER 22 —

LEARNING THE VALUE
OF FRATERNITY

When one hears the word *fraternity*, it is not uncommon to conjure the thought of a group of young men living and socializing together on a university campus. That particular definition is not what we are focusing on in this chapter; however the terms within the definition of fraternity do indeed apply.

Fraternity is defined as a body of people associated for a common purpose or interest. While that could be a collegiate group it can also apply to several individuals who come together in a "one-ness" of purpose. It is possible that the fraternization is structured and organized. It is also possible that individuals with "like" goals simply gather to achieve the ideology or cause in which they believe.

A sense of fraternity can take on both positive and negative purpose. Our society is well aware of negative fraternization which takes on the image of street gangs. It is obvious they connect with one another as their similarities draw them together. It is also due to the fact that they want to belong and feel a sense of association. It is not uncommon for individuals who affiliate with gangs to have a limited personal history of being invited to participate or attach to anyone or anything that offered them a sense of purpose. And for point of reference, *purpose* can be good or bad. I have had the opportunity to visit with individuals who are gang affiliated and they have told me that their group affiliation is something to which they are more connected than the family in which they were born. In the end, being fraternal with a group that not only doesn't contribute to society but actually causes destruction within it, is still a fraternity of sorts. In this sense, it appears to fill a need they have to unify and belong.

Speaking of unity as we did in the last chapter, let's blend that term with fraternity and place it in a positive community setting.

When people come together for a "one-ness" of purpose and pull together (like the team of horses I referred to in the last chapter illustrating unity) and do so for a common purpose or interest (fraternity), mountains can figuratively and literally be moved.

This nation is blessed with many local, regional, and national non-profit organizations that make the world a better place. Whether it is a small parent group at a local school or a 1.7 million member national organization, when people come together in a sense of fraternity with a productive and positive goal in mind, communities and people improve! When a fraternal group chooses to support the developmentally disabled, elects to assist senior citizens within the neighborhood, offers to build scholarship for financially-disadvantaged youth; it not only helps our society and fellow man but it also becomes contagious. A fraternal effort helping others has a strong tendency to draw in others to assist in the same mission.

Another wonderful thing happens when positive fraternization occurs. The participants focus less on themselves and more on the mission at hand. Thus, participating in an effort of fraternity is a sure way to avoid *Delusional Entitlement Disorder.*

Remember when we blended the concepts of unity and fraternity? Let's add another leg to the three-legged stool of which we spoke earlier in this book. When a sense of charity is added to an effort of unity in a field of people who fraternize in a "one-ness" of purpose, the world improves.

If you are not involved in a positive community group in which you can feel a contribution to a purpose or interest in your life, become involved! Your efforts will touch the lives of many.

— CHAPTER 23 —

WHEN HUMOR ISN'T FUNNY

At some time or another, all people enjoy laughter and humor. It does the self good to have a good laugh and experience a room full of smiles. A good time with humor and laughter included is very beneficial to the mind and body. However, when the so-called humor is pointed to a person or persons it can result in a very painful experience. Sarcastic and *put-down* comments made in an attempt at being humorous is not actually funny. At least for one person with that individual being the brunt of the joke.

We have all experienced it. There is usually at least one in each crowd, one in each workplace, or one in each family. They insult someone in the name of humor and do so by making fun of something the other person did, announcing something embarrassing about a person in the group, or ridicule them in a laughing manner.

As it relates to this book, the characteristics of *entitlement* (the person making the sarcastic comments feel that they are entitled to make fun of others) and *delusion* (somewhere in the conscious or subconscious core of the sarcastic humorist they are confident of their superiority over the person they are insulting and perceive that their comments are funny). When sarcastic and insulting humor occurs, several other things happen:

- *At first, the other people present seem to laugh along with the alleged joke which magnifies the negative impact to the victim.*
- *At the onset, the victim of the humor may play along and try to laugh it off in an attempt to minimize the event and move on.*
- *At some point, others can see the victim transition from playing along to experiencing irritability and frustration. This migrates into their sense of the need for the victim to retaliate against the person who insulted them. The individual who was being slighted by the quasi-humorous comments and was passively defensive now goes on the offensive against the person who started this insulting bantering.*
- *About this time, the crowd who initially laughed along now begins to feel uncomfortable. They often attempt to change the subject.*
- *However, the bristling caused by the insulting and sarcastic attempt at humor has taken on a toxic effect. The end result could be days, weeks, months or years of bitterness between people especially the insulter and the victim.*

Laughter at the expense of another is damaging. And it goes a bit deeper. It has often been said that there is a lot of truth in comments that are made in jest. This type of dysfunctional humor not only incorporates behavior consistent with **D.E.D.**, it often reveals the true sentiment being felt by the person doing the insulting. Whether consciously or subconsciously, it creates a passive manner by which a person who holds some deep seeded distaste or resentment can insult another person in the name of humor. Here is an example:

<u>What Bill Is Saying:</u>	"So Tom, you got a job at the XYZ Company? What is your job?....scrubbing the restrooms?"
<u>What Bill Is Thinking:</u>	(I applied for work at the XYZ Company and wasn't hired. Even though Tom has a degree in engineering, I think I am much smarter that Tom and should have been given a job there before him. I really am jealous and don't like Tom.)

Sarcastic and insulting humor is not only lacking true entertainment, it is also highly contagious. In a family, workplace, social gathering where insult humor is present, it typically becomes more frequent among its members. A person who has been insulted by humor will have a propensity to use insult humor to retaliate or gain a sense of power. This creates a domino effect and can ruin any positive attitude that has resided within that group.

Sarcastic and insulting humor not only creates friction and negative reaction, it also meets the criteria for **Delusional Entitlement Disorder.**

— CHAPTER 24 —

GOING BEYOND THE BASICS

In the early 1980's, I was doing a rotation courtesy of the U. S. Navy at a veteran's hospital in Florida. It was a lazy late Sunday morning. Our team had circulated throughout the rooms and hallways that were filled with men and women who had served their country well during some of the direst times of this nation's history.

A lively and energetic Navy nurse named Ginny suddenly popped into the break room where we were sipping coffee.

"Doc Shock (*my nickname which has stuck with me through my professional career*) get me a can of shaving cream, after shave, lipstick and fingernail polish," the Lt. Commander ordered, " We are going to doll-up these guys and gals."

For the next 4 hours, we shaved the men and painted the fingernails of the ladies. I met gentlemen who had been on the beach at Normandy, in the ships at Pearl Harbor as well as those who fought in the jungles of Southeast Asia, met women who had flown support aircraft, and been introduced to former military nurses who had tried to relieve the pain of the soldiers who were suffering the impact of napalm. Their histories were incredible.

The conversation, laughter and proverbial story-telling ran rampant that afternoon amongst these noble men and women.

As we were completing our day, Nurse Ginny walked up to me and said, "Shock, there are people in this world who feel they are entitled who have offered very little to their neighbors. They live in a dream world that tells them they are owed something. Now these ladies and gentlemen fought for the freedom we enjoy. They don't ask for praise. All they ask for is their dignity. Today, they are entitled to feel good about themselves and we have done just that. And that almost makes us worthy to be in the same room as them."

A sense of contentment came over our unit that afternoon as we concluded our duty. It came to our attention that not one of us had spent any time focusing on our own concerns and problems.

In essence, we had participated in the antithesis of **Delusional Entitlement Disorder**. We had served our fellow mankind and grown personally because of our experience.

As we left that afternoon and were walking out of the wing of the hospital, a retired Marine stood at the doorway of his hospital room. Missing a left arm and right leg, he propped himself up in the doorway. With a salute of his one remaining upper extremity, he bellowed down the hall "Attention on deck!"

We could hear applause from some of the patient rooms. We listened as several veterans' shouts of gratitude echoed down the hall.

As our team walked silently onto the elevator with a lump in each one of our throats, we understood the triangulation of charity, unity and fraternity.

We truly comprehended the opposite of what someday would be termed *Delusional Entitlement Disorder.*

— CHAPTER 25 —

MEDIA TOXICITY

I won't deliver a sermonette on the amount and degree of violence, treachery, deception, deceit, and dishonesty that is represented on television and in entertainment media today. The subject has been tossed around substantially. What can be said is that while there is a constellation of excellent educational and entertainment programming available, the magnitude of negative and harmful broadcasting is measurable. A few years ago, I appeared as a guest psychotherapist on a regional network show in which they were surveying children from ages 12 to 17 regarding how much television they watched in an average day. The usual response was at least 5 hours per day even on school days. Most of those hours fell within highly-dramatic, violent, and manipulative content.

Being a teenager in the 1960's, I watched the migration of lyrics in popular music become more descriptive and confrontational to healthy boundaries over the years. How often it is that you see a child, adolescent or young adult with a music listening device in their ears as they go about their activities. A recent survey noted that young people from the ages of 12 to 17 absorb approximately 10 hours of music per day. Again and in parallel with the comment about television and visible media, there is a large volume of entertaining and uplifting music on the airwaves along with the tunes that advocate violence, treachery, deception, deceit, and dishonesty. And the latter group is so damaging.

The same goes for what is accessible on the computer. Educational materials co-exist with a high level of internet trash.

Quite noticeable in the contaminated side of the media are the advertisements that suggest unless you possess certain material goods, your self-worth is less. In the musical lyrics, too often intimations of violence and disrespect for others form the theme for the song in a *take what you want from other people* mentality. To achieve a thrilling story line, many series on both television and movies resort to violence, sexual denigration, murder, and greed. These types of media content combine to form disharmonious underpinnings that suggest to the recipient:

- *You deserve the best*
- *You deserve it free*
- *You deserve it now*
- *Somebody owes you*
- *You have the right to do what you want*
- *You have the right to take things from others*

Oh wait! In part, those bullet notes form the subtitle of this book! That would suggest that the toxic media exposure advances the cause of *Delusional Entitlement Disorder.*

Theories exist in human behavior that tout the fact that dysfunctional media saturation is occurring within the developmental years of our children, adolescents and young adults. Thus it is very safe to opine that the greater the exposure to harmful media, the greater the potential for development of *Delusional Entitlement*

Disorder and thus the greater frequency of this unofficial disease's emergence into our communities.

The concern of media toxicity is not reserved for the minors in our society. Adults invest a lot of time impregnating their minds with the same level of destructive entertainment. A very interesting observation is to watch attitudes in a person become altered after they watch a certain type of programming. How often it is that a person adopts the attitude parallel to what they were watching.

Media exposure within itself can be addictive and distractive. I have heard numerous accounts of how parents and siblings can't be disturbed when they are watching their favorite shows, listening to their favorite music or participating in a website or video game with which they are enthralled.

Here is an antidote to toxic media exposure:

- *Turn the device off*
- *Read a book.*
- *Go outside and engage in health-driven activities with the family*

Volunteer at a local charity; get a dose of life and reality

By doing so, **D.E.D.** has a lesser chance of infecting you and your family.

— CHAPTER 26 —

KARMA

The use of the word karma in this chapter should be viewed as a term with a small "k" and not capitalized if that is possible. It is my intent to use the definition as one of action as it relates to cause and effect and not a part of Eastern theophilosophy.

The dictionary defines karma as an understanding that *if you do good things, good things will happen to you – if you do bad things, bad things will happen to you."* We also view this as the golden rule. It is also quoted as *doing things to others as you would have them do to you.* One frequent saying regarding this theory is *what goes around...comes around.*

The act of karma is critically important when dealing with **D.E.D.** If people were to view their attitudes and actions from the perspective of what seeds they sow with mankind determine what harvest they reap for themselves, there would be less **D.E.D.**

Let's look for a moment at how *Delusional Entitlement Disorder* and our use of the word *karma* relate.

Let's say that a person is known to treat their neighbors with condescension, arrogance, and criticism. Perhaps they choose to speak ill of people within their community and do so with venom and insult. Furthermore, they may employ gossip which can trigger a firestorm of murmuring by others. They can go so far as to create an assassination of the verbally-battered person's integrity and character. But let them be the brunt of criticism and embarrassment and they are quick to cry foul.

I was speaking with a retired judge a few years ago who was reflecting on his years in the practice of law and time spent on the bench. His comment was this, "In all my years dealing with conflict whether it is civil or criminal, I am still amazed at how many people ignore that they are usually reaping the results of the seeds they themselves planted. Yet they are quick to blame everyone except themselves. Call it karma, call it what goes around comes around. Repeat criminal offenders, repeat divorce cases, and those that continue to harm others...simply don't get it."

A farmer named Ralph was digging in the soil at his farm checking the growth of his planted crops. He looked at me and noted, "I am always amazed at how a person can plant seeds and they grow into crops just by nature itself. Planting seeds and having them grow into crops is a miracle from God but a lot of people don't think of it that way. Life is like that too. If people just planted more good seeds the world wouldn't be in so much turmoil."

Albert is a gentleman from upstate New York. He owned a service station for several years. Albert could quickly tell you the difference between a gas station and a service station. With the latter, the attendant actually provided services for the customer including pumping their fuel, checking the level of motor oil, inflating a low tire, and cleaning the windshield. I speculate that many readers don't have a recollection of an actual service station. Albert's level of service didn't stop there. He always had lollipops for the children accompanying their parents. He knew his customers by name and knew their families. He invested the time it took to answer questions and if he didn't know the answer at that moment, he would research it and advise them later. Retired and in his senior years, numerous residents of this town will approach Albert calling him by name and letting him know how they fondly remember him. Albert planted seeds early on with his hospitality, courtesy, and kindness. He didn't do it with an ulterior motive in mind. As karma would have it, he is blessed in his senior years with respect, kindness, and courtesy in the same proportion he handed out with those lollipops, service, and a smile.

This brings us to another term that was briefly alluded to in Albert's story. Intent. If you recall, we also talked about intent back in Chapter Fourteen.

All of us have met someone who does favors with the intent of getting something in return. All of us have actually done it, whether knowingly or unknowingly. Offering a gift of fellowship, good deed, courtesy, or lending a helping hand is to be done in the true form of charity of which we spoke earlier in this book. Lending a helping hand and planting a good seed without anticipation of return on investment is what good karma is all about.

Two men were once talking about a third person that had harmed them immensely. The first man noted all the despicable acts this person had done and all the harm they had caused.

"I can't wait until his karma catches up with him. He is such a jerk! I am looking forward to watching him get his just due," the first man said.

The second man softly replied, "That isn't how karma or whatever you call it works. Your wishing justice and vengeance on this person can be just as bad as his actions. You should be forgiving him for what he has done to you and move on in life without anger. By doing so, you plant the seeds of goodwill or good karma. For whatever he is held accountable to is between himself and a supreme being."

It is good that all of us go out into the world and plant good seeds.

— CHAPTER 27 —

BECOME A VOLUNTEER!

The teenagers were cranky. They were bored. It was a Wednesday afternoon in late November. School had been dismissed for 5 days. Their friends had left town with their parents for the brief holiday. There was nothing on television they liked and they were tired of their video programs.

The man of the house was grouchy. During the days the family had off from school and work the weather was damp and chilly. It was lousy golf weather.

The lady of the house was in a relatively good mood until she started to absorb the attitudes of the children and her husband. It wasn't that they were being nasty. They wanted to be entertained and that simply wasn't happening.

"We should do something different and exciting," she cheerfully said.

"You find something different and exciting to do and I am on-board with you," said the father.

"Heck yeah Mom, find something for us to do. It is so boring here in this house. We are tired of this place," one teenager chided in.

For point of perspective in accordance with the comment by the teenager referencing their boring house, the family lived in a 4,500 square foot home. Each child had their individual bedroom with incredible decor, the residence was equipped with modern conveniences in the kitchen and family room, and a hot tub sat on the back deck that faced the beautiful mountains.

Now back to the story. The mother thought for a while as she puttered around the house. So her spouse and children were bored, eh? She departed from the room and spent time on the telephone soon returning with a grin on her face.

Later that evening she announced to the family that they had to arise early the next day because she had a surprise for them. They were both puzzled and excited.

The following day was Thursday. It was Thanksgiving Day. They were up and ready early that morning. Of course, dad and teenagers were eager to find out what they were doing differently that day.

"Well, you know we have been invited to the Baker's house for Thanksgiving dinner later today, but I have us signed up to do something different this morning," she cheerfully stated, "We are going down to the mission and help prepare and serve a Thanksgiving meal to those who have no family and have no place to go."

The look on the faces of the three family members was of shock. There was some less-than-warm discussion that bantered back and forth, but within the hour they were in the car on the way to the mission.

Within a couple of hours, both children were stirring large pots of mashed potatoes, the husband was busy slicing turkey and the mother was helping set out paper plates along with the other approximately 50 volunteers that were there that day.

What the mother remembers to this day is the laughter she could hear emanating from her daughters as they flung potatoes on the paper plates as they went down the make-shift assembly line. She also recalls the conversation between her smiling husband and each disadvantaged person that passed by as her spouse ensured they had gotten enough to eat.

Several years have passed. Both daughters, now adults, are involved in human services careers…helping others. The husband is on the board of one of the local charities but still has time for family, work and recreation. The mother spends a lot of time involved with the same activities as her spouse. The joy of serving others in the form of volunteerism made them a better family so says all of them.

To offset the potential for getting caught up in the *it's all about me* syndrome and to avoid exposure to **D.E.D.,** become involved in your community as a volunteer. It offers you the opportunity to give back to your community without assigning a dollar sign of income to your effort.

It also affords you the blessing of being able to help mankind. It also provides a way of expressing your appreciation for all that you have. If you don't think you have blessings for which to be thankful, spend a few hours volunteering for the disadvantaged and you will rapidly become acquainted with those who suffer more than you. What you will receive from your volunteering is difficult to put into words. It changes your perspective from a mental, emotional, physical and spiritual view.

Teach your children to volunteer for projects in your community. There are a large number of them in each and every neighborhood. If you want to be a contributor to society, invest some volunteer hours. The experience may inoculate you from getting *Delusional Entitlement Disorder.*

— CHAPTER 28 —

THE TEAPOT

I heard a man tell a story about a teapot. He gave an account as to how his grandmother kept a worn teapot on a shelf in her kitchen. It was dented and discolored. He told how he would make fun of the old teapot which resulted in her giving him a smile and simply shaking her head. Although his grandmother had newer appliances including a stainless steel teapot, she would periodically take down the old battered one for the purpose of fixing a hot beverage.

The gentleman told me that it was several years before he discovered the significance of the old teapot. Although it was old, battered, dented, and discolored it could still hold water, carry tea and serve others. And therein defines its value.

The old teapot is a similitude to the aging population and its value despite the worn appearance. Senior citizens reside within our communities and we too often view them as simply sitting on the shelf. We notice that they appear battered, dented, and tarnished. We also have a tendency to underestimate their value and what they can offer.

Just think of the stories that old teapot could tell. And then consider the stories, experiences, and wisdom that the older generation can offer. We often view the old teapots in this world as tarnished when our observation should be that the vessel is well-seasoned. This is why I have tried to replace the word *older people* with *seasoned people.*

A sure way to reduce the frequency of **Delusional Entitlement Disorder** is to spend more time with the seasoned teapots in our communities. When we invest time, attention, and energy into our senior population, it has a tendency to re-center us. Not only do we learn to appreciate what they can hold and what they can carry, we also learn to honor how they can still serve others.

When children are taught to honor their *seasoned* relatives and the elder population of the community, they learn the characteristics of compassion. Those lessons carry through to the adult years. Where compassion for others exist especially for the senior citizens of our society, the entitlement appears to be less. When we spend time with our elder relatives and community residents, it results in a dose of centered reality that has a strong tendency to displace delusional thinking.

— CHAPTER 29 —

PARENT- TO- CHILD D.E.D.

As the family sat in my office for counseling, I could see one of the older children seething with anger. As psychotherapists often do, I reconfigured the appointment which permitted me to spend some one-on-one time with the young girl.

"You seem angry", I asked the 11-year old, "do you mind sharing what is making you upset?"

Most willingly she blurted out, "I hate my parents!"

As a psychotherapist, I knew that there are commonly two populations of children that make that statement. The first group is comprised of youngsters who simply resent being held to a disciplinary standard. They make the absurd statements of contempt against their parents while in their childhood and then appreciate the accountability taught to them when they later have children of their own.

The second group is constructed of children who have been exposed to some form of abuse or compromise to their integrity. I was soon to find out that this young girl belonged to the latter population.

"My parents sleep in every morning. My brother, sister, and I have to get ourselves ready for school. I make the lunches for my brother, sister, and me. It is always peanut butter sandwiches. When we ask for help in the morning they scream and tell us to shut up," she noted, "In the evening they sit around watching television. My dad goes out with his friends and sometimes my mom goes out with her friends and they don't come home until after we have gone to bed. When we want something to eat, they usually tell us to go get something at the convenient mart across the street or order a pizza."

My first impulse was to agree with the young girl that she had a reason to feel anger and frustration. My second notion was to find out more about this family.

In a subsequent visit with the young girl and her brother, I discovered that the father was on disability but certainly had the time, ability, and energy to go four-wheeling with his friends and play golf periodically. Their mother was receiving unemployment compensation. According to the children, mom had been hired and fired at least twice in the past few years and knew how to obtain unemployment rather easily.

The family history that unfolded during my interaction with the entire family included the fact that the man and woman both were college educated and held multiple occupational skills. They had manipulated their status in order to qualify for governmental food subsidy. It was also discovered by a slip-of-the tongue by one family member that the parents would procure food with their food subsidy benefits and then sell them to their friends at a reduced price giving them cash spending money.

After a few visits with the family, I invited the mother and father into my office to discuss recommendations on improving their family structure. When I recommended that they adopt better daily schedules that permit them to spend more time with their children in a responsible fashion, they both responded with an eye-roll and a smirk. When I asked them to consider returning to some form of daily productivity which could include employment for the purpose of improving their family resources as well as offer their children a more responsible example, they promptly fired me and walked out of the office. A few days later, I was advised by our business office that the check they gave us for professional services had bounced.

This is a prime example of parents tutoring their children in the art form of **Delusional Entitlement Disorder.**

For point of clarity, let me state that I have a great appreciation for programs such as food subsidy, unemployment insurance and disability benefits. That is, as long as they are used honestly.

For decades upon decades we have been advised that children learn from examples offered by their parents. From theories within behavioral science we are advised how impressionable our youth are in development years. When you look at the story just told to you, one recognizes the horrific message sent to these children by their entitled parents. Sadly, it is within a high probability that some if not all of those children will adopt at least some of the **D.E.D.** patterns exhibited by their parents.

Too often, parents who do not invest the energy into their children's true needs force the children to become *parentified* (adopting responsibility of parenthood while they are still in their youth). How often we have seen children assuming responsibility for parents not because they are disabled but because they are irresponsible.

Even more distressful is the fact that the story told to you occurs more frequently than we would hope. Over the years, teachers have told me how disheartening it is to see an increasing number of children coming to school with the signs of dysfunctional parenting similar to this story. The teachers and I agreed that two major characteristics that continue to surface are a *sense of entitlement* and a *thought process that certainly wasn't realistic or responsible.*

The product from such parental attitudes is children who grow into adults and employ the same *Delusional Entitlement Disorder.* lifestyle. *D.E.D.* in parenting is not always intentional or malicious. It can be the result of a trickle-down lifestyle to which they have become accustomed or were taught in their youth.

To avoid the phenomenon of parents teaching their children *D.E.D.,* the following is recommended:

- *Teach children by actual example not by yelling instructions or delegating responsibility to others.*
- *Demonstrate a pattern of a useful day. Be productive.*
- *Be a responsible parent. Don't try to be your child's buddy. While youthful vigor is wonderful to share with a child, don't lose your role as a responsible parent.*
- *Teach the value of the balance between work and play. Both are vital to a joyful life.*
- *Stop relying on government and social program to provide for the family when the same can be achieved by one's own effort.*

Planting the seeds of good spirit, good responsibility, good moments of learning and good effort among a family, results in the harvest of children who contribute to themselves as well as society.

— CHAPTER 30 —

BROKEN DOWN

A few years ago, I was speaking with a man and his wife who shared an extraordinary experience with me.

This gentleman, we will call him Jim, was a wholesale marketer of children's toys. Jim and his spouse were in the business of toy sales in a multi-state region. How they facilitated their territory was rather unique as well.

Jim and his wife owned a large motor home. This permitted them to travel throughout their assigned multi-state area and call on their customers while having their transportation and housing in one comfortable unit. They used one of the sleeping areas within the motor home to house hundreds of toys and games they would use as samples for the toy store owners.

Jim told me how they were driving through a rural area in the central states when a mechanical problem with their vehicle occurred. It was on a Friday preceding a holiday weekend. Within the small town they neared was a service station with one mechanic. Although the mechanic had never serviced a motor home of this make and style, he rapidly identified the engine part that was defective. That was the good news. The less than good news was that the only replacement part was in Kansas City approximately 600 miles from them. He would order the part and it would be shipped by the following Tuesday.

The reality of being broken-down in this small community for a period of 5 days soon set in. The weather was dry and hot. The service station owner invited them to park their unit behind his shop. Jim and his wife were arranging themselves to make the best of a bad situation in their stalled motor home when a knock came at the door.

It was the service station owner who held in his hand one end of a heavy-duty extension cord for them to pull needed electricity from his service station. This was soon followed by a local resident, who they had not yet met, with a platter of food and a pitcher of lemonade. Shortly thereafter, a third knock announced the presence of another local resident asking if there was anything else they needed.

By mid-day Saturday they had been introduced to a number of new friends from that community. By Saturday night, there were additional community members along with Jim and his wife sitting in lawn chairs next to the disabled motor home telling stories and sharing ice cream.

An additional greeting was at the door on Sunday afternoon. Another resident was inviting them to a holiday picnic that would occur on Monday less than ¼ mile from where their motor home was stranded. They graciously accepted the invitation.

When noon came on that holiday Monday, what Jim and his wife witnessed touched them deeply. They were invited to join the other area residents around several tables that were constructed in the shaded backyard of one of the neighbors. The food and beverage was plentiful. So was the laughter and warm attitude. There must have been fifty to sixty people there with half of them being children.

With no advanced signal prior to the meal an older gentleman stood and gave thanks for all their blessings. Without any prompting, the men young and old removed their hats and all bowed their heads as the blessing of the food was offered. There was no hoopla. It wasn't dramatic. There was no wailing, shouting or theatrics. It was simple and sincere.

As the food was passed, the older children helped the younger children with their food. It was also obvious to Jim and his wife that the manners they were observing weren't being exhibited in a manner designed to impress anyone. Their manners were a routine occurrence.

Jim and his wife were so impressed and appreciative as they whispered back and forth for a moment trying to deduce a method by which they could show appreciation. Jim asked one of the parents if he and his wife could offer some gifts to the children to which the individual and other adults were most receptive.

They went back to the motor home and gathered a variety of toys from their stash in the storage room and then returned to the picnic area. Upon their arrival, the man who had blessed the food stood and said, "Kids, these nice folks have something for each of you."

The children lined up with the older ones ensuring that the younger kids were in line in front of them. There was no pushing or shoving. No screaming by child nor directives shouted by parent. Each youngster gladly received a toy from Jim and his wife with a smile on their face. They didn't examine the toy to determine if they liked it. They simply took it and were thankful. There was no haggling over someone getting a better toy than another.

Jim told me he how amazed he was with the level of maturity and gratitude exhibited by this group. The mechanical part arrived that following Tuesday morning and was installed in their motor home making it functional. They left later that day to return home. As Jim said, "We left that area with a lot less toys in our vehicle but with a greater understanding in ourselves."

What was missing in that community was *delusional attitude* and demands of *entitlement*. What was present in that part of America was a glimpse of pioneer spirit. It existed in both young and old.

— CHAPTER 31 —

D.E.D. BY OSMOSIS

The parent stormed into the police department demanding to speak to the person in charge. The desk officer informed the parent that she was the officer in charge. The parent began to scream at the officer with profanity and attitude. When the desk officer asked the parent to please lower the voice and a more civil tone, the parent demanded to speak to the desk officer's supervisor.

The supervisor soon emerged and began to visit with the irate parent. Immediately, the parent advised the supervisor that the desk officer is a rude (expletive) and then proceeded to demand why their son is being picked on by the police.

After reviewing data in the computer the supervising officer informed the parent that their son was cited for driving recklessly through a school zone where he almost struck small children in what appeared to be an attempt to impress his friends who were riding with him.

With a blistering scream the parent retorted, "Oh yeah? Well I am going to have somebody's badge! I don't care how many (expletive) witnesses you think you have, my son wouldn't do that!"

The parent turned to the son who has been standing in the background and says, "Don't worry honey, we'll get you a good attorney and make them look like fools."

The young man offered a sneer at the officer and swaggered out of the police station with his parent.

Across town, a shaking and terrified third grader sobbed as she told her mother about the frightening experience with the careening car that almost struck her and her friends.

A few chapters ago, we discussed how parents can establish standards for their children that aren't good when it comes to a sense of entitlement and delusional (I am better than others) thought. The example we used was in the restaurant where the parents chose to re-arrange the tables regardless of the disruption it caused others. I suggest that is an example of a *poor example*. The story that began this chapter is not only true, it is a prime illustration of direct and destructive teaching. When direct indoctrination of **D.E.D.** occurs, it's as if it transferred from one person to another by osmosis.

The parent in the police station missed a wonderful opportunity to teach the son the significance of [a] respecting others, [b] being compliant with the law, [c] maintaining good manners, and [d] being held responsible for one's action.

In my role as a psychotherapist, I cannot even begin to count the number of times that an individual has revealed remorse not for their mistake but for getting caught and not being able to outsmart the authorities through deception and fraud. When adults adopt this feature of *Delusional Entitlement Disorder*, it is almost certain that they have taught the same direct and destructive behavior to others within their family.

When I was a sophomore in high school I made some rather unflattering and insulting remarks about a girl who had just moved into our neighborhood. In my attempt to *be cool* and gain popularity among my peers, I offered insults about the way this girl dressed and remarks about her weight to a group of my friends. My comments filtered back to the girl who informed her father about what I had said.

One afternoon I walked into the house to find my father sitting at the dining room table. He wasn't smiling.

"What can you tell me about the new girl that moved in down the street?" he asked.

"Oh, she dresses funny and is kinda fat. The guys and I were having a good laugh about her." I replied.

(Now this is an interesting fabrication on my part. There were no other guys making fun of her, there were no other guys laughing, it was simply me insulting someone and trying to make it appear that I had an entourage that agreed with me.)

"Well, I hope you can explain the humor when we go down to her house and explain your comments to the girl and her father" he said.

After the blood drained out of my face and slowly returned, I broke into a cold sweat. That was indeed the most painful trek I had ever made as my father and I drove o the new girl's house. As we walked into the residence, I noticed how bare the rooms were. The girl's father was very polite but I could easily see the disgust he held for me. With blushing face and head held low, I apologized to the young lady and her father. Her father told me that they had moved to the community to get a new start after the girl's mother had died and he had lost his job. He let me know that it was his daughter's hope that she could make new friends and fit into the school and neighborhood. I could hardly breathe.

And then the young girl Carolyn, did the most dignified thing. She held out her hand and said, "Ed, I accept your apology".

The short drive back to our house was heart-wrenching for me. My father had held me accountable. Dad had insisted that I apologize and make things right. That really hurt because it collapsed the delusional and arrogant air of entitlement I had cultivated. But what a lesson it was. I have reflected on that experience repeatedly over the past decades. What a valuable teaching moment it was. I praise any parent who offers their child the same accountability. What my father gave me was the antidote to **D.E.D.** by osmosis.

— CHAPTER 32 —

ANOTHER VIEW FOR
A HEALTH PLAN

As this book goes to print our nation is in a blistering discussion regarding healthcare. A proposal for national healthcare for all citizens has been made. Some people feel that healthcare should be free and available to all citizens within the United States. Others opine that Americans should assume responsibility to procure their own healthcare provisions. Some sense that insurance companies are to blame. Others place fault with the legal community for being over-zealous with malpractice claims. Another group points to governmental control as the culprit.

One thing that has proven itself over time is that when an individual is required to invest in their own healthcare they take it more seriously and are more likely to improve their own well-being. Conversely, when healthcare requires no investment the individual often does not approach it as seriously. They often abuse the system and expect others to assume responsibility for them.

So why, you may ask, are we discussing healthcare in the context of this book on *Delusional Entitlement Disorder*? It is because there is an aspect of healthcare entitlement that is not getting much discussion during this political time.

An innovative aspect of American healthcare that should be touted is:

Take better care of yourself and invest daily in preventive measures. Live a healthier lifestyle, assume responsibility for eating properly, adopt better sleeping patterns, avoiding risky habits, exercise more with the family, and learn more about what can help you maintain good health that precludes you from having to go through as much "damage control" at the doctor's office or the hospital.

This responsibility is not limited to the average individual. If government wants to get involved in healthcare they should place more emphasis and education on staying healthy. If corporations want greater productivity and employee satisfaction they should place more emphasis and education on staying healthy in the workplace. If communities wish to become less disease and illness prone they should emphasize wellness at the same magnitude as disease repair.

Of course, much of the responsibility does indeed rest with the individual and within the family. By eating less junk food, by reducing the amount of "fast foods", by taking the time to prepare healthy meals (*which is actually less costly than dining out or purchasing fast food*), by turning off the television and participating in activity, by reducing unhealthy health-risk habits, and by taking advantage of the free information on wellness that is available everywhere; individual and family wellness can be achieved.

Individuals who choose to live an unhealthy life while expecting the healthcare system to make them well are engaged in *Delusional Entitlement Disorder*.

People who have elected to assume responsibility for their own physical, mental, and emotional wellness have a greater immunity from ***D.E.D.***

Some of you may be asking whether this approach to self-responsibility for healthcare violates the premise of charity for those who are ill and in need. It does not. Unquestionably, there are individuals who take good care of themselves and strive for optimal health who still contract severe illness or suffer serious injury. As caring Americans we should extend our efforts of compassionate works whenever it is necessary. That doesn't excuse an individual or family from striving to improve their health and wellness through an investment in better living.

The difference between *ignorance* and *stupidity* was explained to me at an early age. The explanation was never meant to be scientific but certainly is practical. There is nothing embarrassing or belittling about being ignorant. It simply means that a person does not know something and has not been taught or exposed to a particular subject. On the other hand stupidity exists when a person has been taught, shown, indoctrinated, educated, or trained in something that makes his or her life better yet they choose to not take advantage of that insight. They keep repeating the same behavior and getting the same maladaptive result.

The approach to American healthcare in this text is simple. Do everything you can to make yourself and your family healthier. Take the initiative to learn all you can about wellness. Promote wellness education in your community, churches, and schools. Simultaneously when you meet someone who is in need and their health is suffering, exercise your efforts of charity and compassion to help your fellow citizen.

This approach to wellness and healthcare defies the presence of ***Delusional Entitlement Disorder.***

— CHAPTER 33 —

CUSTOMER SERVICE

If you are a company owner or the proprietor of a business, please invest some time explaining customer service and business etiquette to your employees. *Delusional Entitlement Disorder* has dug its claws into the business world and it rears it ugly head in the form of lacking customer courtesy and service.

Perhaps it is my migration toward the age of 60 that is having some impact, but if I am called "dude" one more time by a checker in the grocery line, I am going to scream. Okay, perhaps I am getting a little more sensitive as I enter that pre-senior citizen category. Let's talk about the more serious matters at hand.

I have spoken to a number of business managers whose stories continue to amaze me as to the number of employees, young and old, who simply walk off the job when they are asked to do something against their preference. Several of these managers advise me it isn't simply walking off the job but also that it is done with a vulgar gesture and foul language. The various managers also inform me that it is done in a spirit that suggests an abnormally high level of arrogance, entitlement and perception of superiority.

A couple of years ago, I was talking to a regional manager of a hardware store who advised me that all of the stores under his purview were running specials on a certain product. The added benefit was that a portion of the sale of that particular product would comprise a donation to a local charity. He further advised me that if I went to one of his stores to ask the clerk for the discount and if there was any problem to simply remind the employee of the special that was being offered in the region.   Indeed, I went to one of his stores and purchased one of the items of which he had advised me was on special pricing. When I approached the checkout stand, the clerk was sitting on top of the conveyor belt, had a music device in both ears to which he was singing along, was munching on part of an sandwich that was sitting next to the cash register and last but not least offered me a well-noticed eye roll when my presence forced him to get down off of the counter and wait on me.

"How's it goin' dude?" was his greeting. I muddled through the greeting but what came next was beyond anything I could imagine. When he totaled my purchase and it was much more than the special pricing, I questioned him.

"I was visiting with your regional manager and he told me that these items were thirty percent off this week", I said.

"Well I don't know nuthin' about that. This is what the register says and that is what I need to charge you", he muttered as he took another bite of sandwich. The music device was still in his ears.

"Could you please check on the price? Mr. Smith (not his real name) assured me there was quite a discount," I asked.

"Hey man, I told you what the price was. If Mr. Smith has something going on maybe he should get his butt down here and take care of this himself. I mean, he makes ten times the money I make and I gotta stand here and take this?" he verbally assaulted me.

Not only have I never returned to that store, I also had the opportunity to speak again with the regional manager. He offered me an apology which was mixed with his advisement that he simply rarely gets quality employees who understand the concept of serving the customer with kindness, professionalism, and courtesy.

What this young man and many others in customer service (or the lack thereof) have developed is *Delusional Entitlement Disorder*. They are the first to complain when there is a staff reduction at their work because business has declined. They are also the first to complain if they are asked to exert a little more effort. It is common to consider that how an entitled employee acts at work is also the manner in which he or she conducts themselves within their home.

The conduct of this type of employee is particularly shocking to those seasoned employees who still understand the importance of customer service and conduct themselves accordingly.

Bill was a friend of mine in earlier years. His father had built a very successful business and upon his father's retirement Bill would take over the business that had spanned forty years. I recall Bill's sarcastic attitude in his earlier days. I recall him driving through town making crude remarks and exhibiting behaviors that indicated he was better than others. Even in the early years in his father's business, when a customer entered their office Bill would not take his feet off of the desk nor get up and greet the customer. This was a far cry from his father who would arrive each day for work in a suit and crisp shirt, greet friend and customer alike on a first name basis, and drive to the residence of a customer if necessary.

When Bill's father retired and shortly thereafter passed away, Bill assumed full control of the business. The same attitude he exhibited in his teens and early twenties was still present in his adult years. Bill began complaining as to how business was poor and offered several excuses none of which were attributed to his attitude.

When Bill's business was on the verge of faltering, he went to some of his father's long-established customers and asked for their advice. They sharply advised Bill that he had never understood the concept of feeling gratitude for the business his customers brought to him. They pointedly let him know that his arrogance and sense of superiority was quickly destroying the business his father had built.

Bill returned to work the next week with a renewed and redirected spirit. He was invested in his customers and not focused on himself. Bill had experienced a close call with a potentially lethal dose of *Delusional Entitlement Disorder.* Thanks to the community members around him, he was able to overcome the illness. Bill is successful today and ironically using his father's premise of putting the customer first, getting acquainted with those you serve, and making your word your bond.

— CHAPTER 34 —

RONNIE ISN'T STUPID

As a young boy, I watched a community come together to propel a young man from obscurity to excellence. The young man's name was Ronnie.

I first became aware of Ronnie at a local function. While the other children were scurrying around at the Easter Egg Hunt, Ronnie was just standing around staring off into space holding an empty bag. A couple of kids felt sad for Ronnie as he stood there looking stupid, so they put a couple of their recovered eggs in his bag. When it came time to see who had gathered the most festively-colored eggs, an adult leader checked Ronnie's bag.

"Did you find some eggs Ronnie?" she asked.

"Somebody put some eggs in my sack," Ronnie mumbled quietly.

Ronnie didn't do well in school. He just sat there. He could never complete any of his assignments. His response to the teacher's questions was always "I don't know."

Whenever Ronnie's family was in public, he just sat by himself. He would sometimes respond and primitively talk with people but often he sat quietly and stared at the ground.

A community leader asked Ronnie's parents if there was anything that could be done to help Ronnie. The father noted that Ronnie had become quieter, had been sitting by himself more, and needed help doing everything. The father implied that he and his wife had accepted the fact that Ronnie was retarded. The mother noted that Ronnie had gone downhill over the past couple of years.

Ronnie's parents were hard working farmers. Their family consisted of 6 children with Ronnie being the youngest. The parents were not educated and provided for their family by diligently working in the fields every day of the year that weather permitted from sun-up to sun-down. The family rarely came to town. They didn't use the local physician opting to use home remedies due to their financial constraints. They didn't socialize very much due to their heavy work schedule and need to constantly tend to the farm.

Ronnie was attending a softball game one summer day with his siblings. It was a rare event for them to attend events in town. As he sat on the front row of the bleachers, a foul ball careened toward him missing him by inches. He never flinched. One of the parents, a nurse, observed the incident. Having known of Ronnie for a couple of years, the woman realized the revelation she had just discovered.

"Ronnie isn't stupid. He isn't retarded. Ronnie is going blind!" she remarked.

In those days vision testing wasn't routine in the schools. Also in that era, very little was known in the rural communities about eyesight degeneration in children. The local physician, after becoming aware of Ronnie's dilemma, visited with the parents. After they overcame their shock and self-guilt for the misunderstanding of the health status of their son, they gave the doctor permission to examine Ronnie. The town physician confirmed the presence of visual deterioration in Ronnie.

When some of the people in the community heard that Ronnie wasn't *stupid* and that he was going blind, they came together to make provisions for him to be evaluated at the School for the Blind at the state capitol about an hour from their little town.

Ronnie was accepted at the school. The community held fundraisers to help offset the cost of specialized education. Ronnie's parents became more active in the community. The community became more active within itself.

It was Christmas Eve 1959. Ronnie had been gone from the community for over a year. His parents would visit him every weekend but the community had not seen Ronnie. His parents kept the community informed that Ronnie was doing well in school. That is all the community knew. That year, a Christmas Eve service at a local church was beginning right after dusk. A few minutes before the service began, a young man walked into the Church. He was wearing dark glasses and was accompanied by a dog trained to assist the blind. It was Ronnie. When it came time for a scripture to be read, Ronnie came to the front of the Church. There on the pulpit sat a very thick book. It was a Braille Bible. The congregation sat there in total awe as Ronnie read with his fingers, the story of the birth of Jesus Christ. As he smiled looking out over the congregation he could not see, his hands traced the passage imprinted in the book. His voice was strong and his inflection was emotional. Tears of joy flowed freely that evening in the rural parish.

Ronnie wasn't stupid. Ronnie was blind. Ronnie, with the help of the community, had overcome his limitation. The story doesn't stop there. Ronnie attended four years of college followed by three years of law school. After a distinguished career in law, he was appointed to the judicial bench. Judge Ronnie retired from the County Court in the late 90's.

Individuals with **Delusional Entitlement Disorder** do not adapt. They choose to permit others to assume responsibility for them. Communities with **D.E.D.** do not serve their fellow citizen. They go inside and close the door. This community placed the needs of one of its own in front of personal needs and wants. Ronnie took advantage of opportunity which gave him a gift he could give back to society. This is what American pioneer spirit is all about.

— CHAPTER 35 —

GLAD I'M NOT THEM

Ted and Greg were passengers in the back seat of the car being driven by Greg's parents. Greg and Ted had been swimming at the local lake and the parents were giving the kids a ride home. While driving down the highway near their hometown, they came upon a car along side the road with its hood up. A man stood beside the vehicle which had smoke pouring out of the engine compartment.

One of the parents in the front seat calmly said to the other who was driving, "Speed up and don't look. We don't want to have to stop. We have things to do at home."

This must have been a common occurrence within this family because the parent driving the car didn't question the remark. The driver simply sped up. Both adults in the front seat kept their eyes straight forward. About a mile further down the road, the driver took a deep sigh and muttered, "I sure am glad I am not him. That would be a terrible situation to be in."

In his telling me of this story, Ted keenly recalled how deep those comments cut through him as a 15-year old. It made no sense to him at all. While keeping one's family and friends out of harm's way is of great importance and a person can never be too safe around strangers on a roadway, Ted kept asking himself what would have the risk been to simply roll down the window and ask if they could call somebody for him? Also, how difficult could it have been to advise someone at the local auto service center a few miles ahead to send someone out to help?

Instead, this stranded motorist was ignored followed by an utterance of gladness that the adults in the front seat weren't as unfortunate as that man. It certainly was *D.E.D.* in its raw form.

— CHAPTER 36 —

MIMIMIZING ATTITUDE

We all remember the *minimizing attitude* that often was first noticed in elementary or middle school. A child would be proud of an achievement. He or she would choose to share it with his or her friends. There was always some other child of approximately the same age, who would walk up to the group, interrupt everyone and say, "Oh that's nothing, I did better than that. That was so easy, nothing to it! No big deal!"

Unquestionably the troublemaker was using a *put down* comment. But his or her derogatory comment went much further. The rude comment was meant to minimize the other person at the very time they are enjoying something positive with others.

In order to form such a derogatory remark and to actually offer it in such a destructive manner, the person must have a sense of entitlement and thoughts of delusional grandiosity about themselves. Thus, the person offering the putdown or minimizing interruption is a carrier of **Delusional Entitlement Disorder.**

We often see children trying to *one up* each other in what appears to be a type of pecking order or power struggle. However, this phenomenon appears to continue into adulthood and takes on at least one other form within the attitude. When D.E.D. adults, like children, continue to minimize the efforts or achievements of others, their secondary intent is to make their own personal achievements appear superior to those around them. Let me go into this a bit deeper.

Mark (*not his real name*) had a very strong opinion of himself. His parents had inflated his ego most of his life. They had told him that he essentially could do no wrong. Therefore when Mark was faced with a challenge or felt threatened by others he would simply minimize the people around him.

A person can perceive moving up the ladder in two ways: [1] by working hard and excelling, or [2] by minimizing others around you to make you look better while you are merely standing still. Mark chose the latter formula.

Rarely did a day go by at his worksite where Mark didn't insult someone, make fun of their clothing, roll his eyes and chuckle at something they said, or take credit for something of which he had made no contribution. There was a strong suggestion that Mark actually damaged the work of some of his co-workers in an effort to make himself look superlative. As time passed, those that worked with Mark began distancing themselves from him. His comments and actions, which he chose to fuel his false sense of entitlement and delusional perception of self, were making others toxic.

Unfortunately, people can read the truth given enough time. People who spent any time around Mark could see the truth. When this occurred the **D.E.D.** was only affecting Mark. He was delusional about himself and thought of himself as entitled. Sadly but realistically, nobody else did.

Mark was found dead one evening in his car. He had intentionally engaged in self-destructive behavior via carbon monoxide by letting the car run with the garage door closed. In speaking with the pathologist who investigated the incident and who had also procured the family history, he made a simple summary, "It appears this man had been told his entire life that he was perfect and that he was the best at everything to the point he began to believe it. When his tactics of manipulating others to make himself look superior no longer worked and reality hit him, his eroding ego got the best of him. When he no longer could destroy others in order to make himself seem superior, he ended up destroying himself."

Individuals who use *put down* or minimizing comments with others in order to make themselves feel and appear superior to others contract **Delusional Entitlement Disorder**. They also eventually implode.

— CHAPTER 37 —

EXTERNAL TOXIC STRESSORS

In the world of professional counseling, it is not uncommon to spend time with a client helping them to identify their *internal* and *external* stressors.

Theories exist which identify *internal stressor* as those behaviors, experiences, thoughts and emotions that we hold within ourselves that cause stress and conflict. We create our own internal stressors. We all have them. Some of us can manage them better than others. Some individuals can easily identify their internal stressors and make appropriate redirection in their life in order to reduce or eliminate them. Others, sadly, cannot. This requires an investment in psychotherapeutic counseling.

Likewise within the same theory, there is another group of stressors we call *external*. This category includes the environments, social clusters, possible employment situations, music, books, movies and obviously people with whom each one of us come in contact whose toxicity and unhealthy structure rubs off on us. Often, these toxic and unhealthy characteristics stick to us like glue.

The purpose of this chapter is not to force the reader to spontaneously abandon their environment and friends but moreso to be aware of those places, people, and things that expose them to greater unhappiness. After external stressors that compromise a person are identified, the individual can make the necessary changes designed to improve their attitude and function.

It is safe to say that most of us have felt changes in their senses when they are around certain types of people. Can you recall being in close proximity to either a person or in a place that gave you peace, warmth, sense of safety, perception of tranquility, and which simply filled your spirit? It is a common experience for many. Likewise, can you remember when you were around someone or something that made you feel uneasy, "yucky", cold and a bit fearful? Again, many have experienced that as well. A large population of mankind will tell you that feeling you get, either good or bad, is that *small still voice* inside your character which is of divine origin. I believe that to be true on a personal basis.

While we often have that little voice or sensation that offers us a feeling of attraction or repulsion; too many men, women and children become entrapped by toxic stress that they don't see coming. Remember in the early chapters of this book where I gave the illustration in which the flight instructor termed *turning slowly*? That is what often occurs when we are exposed to toxic people, places and things. Our migration toward the toxic external stressor is so slow that we aren't aware we are migrating toward it. While it is good to befriend others and resist judging our fellow man, it is also good to evaluate as to what we can become exposed that can harm us. With this in mind, here are a few helpful hints on how to recognize external toxic stressors:

- *Do you feel worse after being near this person, place or thing? Can you detect yourself becoming more cynical, critical, demanding and irritated?*

- *Would you be embarrassed to tell your family, business associates and those you consider your good and stable friends that you have been associated with this person, place or thing?*
- *Is there a greater potential for violating legal, ethical and moral standards when you spend time with this person, place or thing?*
- *Are your personal goals and values changing (especially slowly) with the more time you invest with this person, place or thing?*
- *Are you spending less time with family, stable friends, and healthy environments (school, church, community service) as you spend more time with this person, place or thing?*

If you answer yes to any of these hints, it is suggested you evaluate your situation and make the appropriate changes. When an individual reduces their exposure to toxic external stressors, they also distance themselves from Delusional *Entitlement Disorder*. As you identify those toxic stressors, don't just abandon everything and run off. Find healthy environments, activities, movies, books, music, social clusters, and new friends to replace that void. You will grow strong very rapidly if you do and you will build more immunity against *D.E.D.*

— CHAPTER 38 —

WHATEVER HAPPENED
TO MANNERS?

When I was in my elementary school years, my mother pulled me aside one day and taught me how to set a table.

"The fork goes here, the knife goes here, the napkin rests here," she said with joy in her voice as she delineated the entire china and stemware setting, "and this is how you use them properly."

I had no joy. This was a waste of my time. I was 8 years old and I had a very busy schedule. There were cartoons to watch!

Nevertheless, I was soon told that it would be my chore to set the table for dinner for the next week. Upon discovering this wimpy assignment that should never be done by a guy in the second grade, I chose to engage in *under the breath muttering* and *covert face making*. As I set the table for that week, I did so begrudgingly with a continuum of muttering and dragging my feet across the floor. Guys weren't supposed to do this. It certainly did not seem to serve any purpose.

I must say that not only was I inundated with table settings, I was also expected to do other ridiculous things such as [a] not chew food with my mouth open, [b] not prop my elbows on the table, [c] not talk with my mouth full, [d] not interrupt others while they were talking, and [e] to use silly terms like "yes sir", "no ma'am", "please", and "thank you" when conversing with others.

And it worsened. By the time I was in the 8th grade, I was taught how to iron clothing and properly take care of my apparel. And if that wasn't bad enough, my father crept into the picture and ensured that I knew how to shake someone's hand, property greet them, and hold the door for a lady. Arrrgghhhh....what was my world developing into?

Interestingly, I recall being invited to various events in my late teens, early twenties and up through the remainder of my adult years thus far in which I needed to know manners, protocol and deportment. Pleasantly, those behaviors were in place because of the parental instruction in my early days.

Because I went through the experience of manners and protocol exercises in my youth, it was felt to be appropriate that the same instructional blessing be bestowed upon my children. Subsequently, many of the same lessons of etiquette were learned by them courtesy of their mother and me. I feel a sense of profound gratitude to my parents for teaching manners that trickled down a generation or three. It is a delight to sit down, dine and socialize with family and friends who know manners, courtesy and protocol. And most of all, interacting with comfort and confidence.

You many inquire as to the significance of manners and social courtesy to the subject of *Delusional Entitlement Disorder?* Where there is structure, comfort, understanding, and standards of behavior there is less chaos and disarray. Furthermore, when people exhibit courtesy and consideration for others, there is less self-centeredness and greed. Where there is less self-centeredness and greed, there is less sense of entitlement and delusional perception of superiority.

Not long ago, my wife sought out current programs by which manners and social deportment could be either taught or reinforced in the wake of increasing societal rudeness. The resources were found to be very limited.

There is a realization that being sloppy and loud is a method of attention-seeking that surfaces much too often. That is why continual reinforcement of appropriate manners and social conduct is vital. People with manners and courteous conduct are recognized as a successful and quality individual. Obviously the opposite conclusion is often reached regarding a person with sloppy and uncouth behavior, absent of manners.

Manners go far beyond dining conduct. One of the most destructive ill-mannered behaviors existing at this time is rude personal phone use. It is much too common to have someone sitting adjacent to you in a restaurant, reception room, in a moving vehicle. and even in a public restroom when their cell phone rings. Not only do they have the volume turned up to an obscene level, they frequently answer it, choosing to talk at a highly intrusive volume sharing their rudeness with others. In our office, we have a sign that requests patients/clients take their cell phone calls out into the central corridor. They still often ignore our request even after being advised verbally as if we are intruding on their rights. And in some instances, they find our request to maintain quiet in our suite an encroachment upon them. One of the most insulting experiences I have personally witnessed recently was during my attendance at a funeral for a friend. During the service at least two cell phones rang. One belonged to an adult who obviously has never heard of turning the ringer to silent. The other ringing cell phone belonged to a teenager who not only answered their phone during the service, but began a conversation. Oh, it gets worse. The parents accompanying the teenager grinned because they thought it was cute. Talking about *Delusional Entitlement Disorder*, we observed two generations functioning under the auspices of *D.E.D.* during one inappropriate phone call.

Whether it is manners during dining, the methods by which we converse and interact, or the inappropriate use of cell phones; manners are lacking. Not only is it refreshing to see families, teenagers, and adults exhibiting good manners and courteous behavior; it establishes a tone of refinement, intelligence, peacefulness, kindness, and harmony when it is used.

One shouldn't restrict their focus on manners to the family and personal setting. Business courtesy and politeness has undergone marked erosion. Rude disrespectful language, destruction of other people's belongings and property, sloppy behavior, highly inappropriate attire, poor hygiene, and unkempt personal care is becoming all too common in the American workplace and business environment. When individuals behave in this manner, it sends a signal of arrogance, ignorance, entitlement, perception of self-centeredness, and apathy to those around them. Often it results in various aspects of business failure. It represents a business model of *Delusional Entitlement Disorder*. Fortunately, there is an excellent resource for polishing business etiquette in today's world.

For the past several years, I have been recommending the words and publications by Jacqueline Whitmore. Ms. Whitmore, the author of "Business Class: Etiquette Essentials for Success at Work", has created a brilliant approach to improving business manners and protocol. Ms. Whitmore is providing the tools for the restoration of class, culture, intelligence, and success in the workplace through improved and courteous conduct. You can view Ms. Whitmore's excellent work at <u>www.etiquetteexpert.com.</u>

In summary, the use of manners is synonymous with success, kindness, intellect, courtesy, and class. The lack of manners to the point of actually believing that sloppy and loud is cute results in *Delusional Entitlement Disorder.*

In the words from a well-known ballad sung by a legendary band, "teach your children well." That goes for manners and courtesy.

— CHAPTER 39 —

SCOUTING AND OTHER ORGANIZATIONS

Organizations exist throughout the United States that are very successful in reducing or eliminating *D.E.D.* in the formative years.

Scouting in America, for both boys and girls, teach principles that render incredible results not only in the youth years but also form fantastic character in adulthood. Scouting teaches a young person how to learn, how to teach others, how to care for their fellow man, how to appreciate charity, how to create unity, and how to develop a sound sense of fraternity. These three characteristics, as you recall, were discussed earlier in this book. Most of all, scouting teaches respect for others and the value of work by example. And furthermore they develop young men and women who are concerned for the welfare of others. Scouting also helps a young person learn how to be responsible. I recommend visiting www. scouting.or or www.girlscouts.org.

Rural and suburban youth organizations exist in which young people are taught to develop leadership, skills for life, citizenship, and learning through experience. One can watch young boys and girls working in agriculture, construction, and animal science all for the purpose of focusing on healthy living and contribution to their communities. Again, they are taught the principles of work and caring for the welfare of others. You may want to look at www.4-h.org.

Thus far in this chapter only youth and adolescents have been mentioned. What about the incredible resources of our senior citizen population? Let's not forget the rich wisdom and knowledge possessed by those who have completed a long career yet in the throes of retirement hold priceless information and know-how that so many people who are junior to them seek. Something wonderful happens when senior citizens participate with organizations and groups that provide opportunity, training, and knowledge for younger or disadvantaged people. The senior citizens, whom I frequently term *seasoned citizens* because they have been well garnished by life experience, combined with others who seek to learn more form an amalgamation that creates community, friendship, and unity, while simultaneously reducing the presence of entitlement and/or delusional sense of self.

I urge parents to expose their children to great youth organizations. I encourage *seasoned citizens* to reach out to the community organizations and volunteer. It will keep your body and mind young and well-lubricated. If you do, you will be amazed at the transformation that will occur.

— CHAPTER 40 —

PATRIOTISM

Not long ago, I participated with the Knights of Columbus in a Veterans Day Parade. When one marches down the parade route an incredible perspective of people can be gained. Our organization carried a set of flags with the United States Flag positioned in the center. As a general rule, the crowd along the sides of the street waved and clapped periodically. However, there were two people that took it a bit further in a touching manner.

An elderly man in a wheel chair was positioned about 5 feet from a young boy who was no more than 4 years old. It was obvious they were not related. They were both simply on the curb of the street. As we approached with the U. S. Flag, the elderly man with great struggle and pain stood from his old and battered wheel chair. He was absent one of his lower extremities. Despite his disability as an amputee, he stood while removing his cap and placing it over his heart. A split second later and without prompting, the small boy snapped a very smart salute with his right hand affixed to his right temple. Two individuals nearly a century apart. Unrelated. No prompting. With automatism that was very natural, they both offered a demonstration of patriotism to the flag of the United States of America. In my heart I wanted to step out of the rank and file, offering gratitude to the older gentlemen who most likely served this great country and further ensured my freedom to march in such a parade. I also wanted to express my gratitude to whoever taught that young child how to show respect for our country's flag.

One of the behaviors some of my friends and I have undertaken in this past few years is to personally thank any military service member with whom we come in contact for their service to this country. An act of gratitude always dilutes any tendency toward entitlement. The look on the faces of uniformed service members after being offered a "thank you" can range from being amazed, to a bit of emotion in the eyes, to devout appreciation for being appreciated.

Parents teach your children the significance of our freedom, the history behind it and the significance of patriotism. The greater the honor to patriotism, the less presence of *D.E.D.* Adults please invest some time in honoring the men and women who served in order to guarantee our freedom as a nation. Again, investing in gratitude and patriotism, significantly reduces the potential for *Delusional Entitlement Disorder.*

— CHAPTER 41 —

BELIEVE IN SOMETHING!

I attended classes offered by a history professor from Indiana University who was colorful in his presentation while being factual in the lessons he taught. His approach to U. S. history was very objective. "Dr. B" was a proponent for the discernment between myth and fact in this country's historical record. He openly discussed the role of faith as it played a large part in the tenacity and motivation of the early pioneers of this country.

I recall as he was leading a discussion on the subject of the role spirituality played within the lives of the early settlers, one student kept muttering, "I don't believe in that." This young man would repeat his statement each time "Dr. B" mentioned another religious sect, spiritual community, or theophilosophy that played a role during the development of this country.

Finally, after hearing the student's constant and repeated comment, "Dr. B" spun on his heals facing the student with a grin on his face and his eyes wide, "C'mon man...you got to believe in something or you yourself are not alive! You can believe in God, trees, Buddha, peanut butter...I don't care...that is the beauty of freedom...you have the privilege and opportunity to have faith in something or someone. You must believe in something!"

After the laughter within the class died down, and the crimson hue to the student's face began to pale, I understood "Dr. B's" teaching point. He certainly wasn't comparing peanut butter to a divine deity. He was simply pointing out that we have the right in this country to have faith in something and exercise it. More importantly, he was teaching us that internally if you do not have some faith precept in your life, you have very little purpose.

Individuals who have very little purpose experience less than favorable motivation. People who lack motivation develop frustration, lethargy, and a problematic attitude. Those who carry a problematic attitude within themselves often try to compensate by becoming bitter, arrogant, manifest a sense of entitlement, and often think with delusion.

To develop in a healthy manner, a person should search inside of themselves to determine what they believe. Then they should explore their inner core in order to identify if they are embracing what they believe in.

One of the most effective mental/emotional exercises that I use in psychotherapy comes from a therapeutic method called, "Task-Enhanced Therapy". I developed the theory along with a physician colleague, Dr. Russell Parker. We then co-authored a book by the same title (*Task-Enhanced Therapy, IUniverse Press, 2007*). In one of the early phases of this therapy, we ask the individual to enter into a quiet retreat with no external stimuli, no distractions, and very little if any interaction with other people. It is not uncommon for that venue to be a small cabin in the mountains or a dwelling along side a small river or creek. Within the confines of this peaceful environment when one is being quiet with their own mind they often become more honest within the self. At the point of self-honesty, one can better define in what they believe. When that inner belief system is defined; it gives a person purpose. When we have purpose and are more familiar in our own core belief values, we have less self-centeredness and offer greater contribution to our communities.

— CHAPTER 42 —

IMPROVING THE FAMILY

The potential for *Delusional Entitlement Disorder* within the family can be reduced if not eliminated by investing in some basic behaviors. When a mother and father implement healthy actions and attitudes, the children are soon to follow. Children believe from an idealistic perspective during the developmental years that their parents are faultless, despite the reality that we are far from that. However, what a parent projects become the standard by which children gauge themselves. When we make good decisions and adopt healthy behaviors, the children attempt to mimic them. When adults exhibit *Delusional Entitlement Disorder*, the children frequently follow the same pathway.

There is a middle ground between being immune from *D.E.D.* and having the impairment in a full-blown condition. That is when we err openly. It is not the fact that we as humans make mistakes. It is what we as adults and parents do with that opportunity. If we simply yell at our children, "Do as I say, not as I do", it sets a very incongruent process within that child. When we make a mistake, acknowledge and correct it, it becomes a prime teaching tool for children to understand that it is human to err yet most wonderful to admit to errors, correct them, and strive to not repeat the behavior. Children admire and emulate such learning experiences.

Here are but a few recommendations designed to improve the family:

- *Watch television less*
- *Look at your children more... eye to eye*
- *Laugh more*
- *Create participation*
- *Demonstrate manners*
- *Reduce complaining and gossiping*
- *Show your children acts of charity*
- *Teach your children how to show respect for others*
- *Hold your children more often*
- *Teach forgiveness by example*
- *Employ discipline and training not to be confused with pure punishment*
- *Exercise as a family*
- *Teach chores in a family by example*
- *Learn about your family heritage*
- *Acquaint the family with your occupation*
- *Invite the immediate and extended family to learn more about your standards and faith*
- *Express appreciation for your children's achievements without placing them on a pedestal*
- *Now that we have talked about children, use the same principles listed above on yourself*

— CHAPTER 43 —

MAKING THE
COMMUNITY STRONGER

Communities are highly contagious. Behaviors and actions of families within a community, good or bad, can spread throughout the neighborhood. It is typical for a family who exhibits happiness, appreciation for others, and success within the family to expand these characteristics to others within the community. Provided they are active among their fellow residents.

Those people plagued with *Delusional Entitlement Disorder* often soften and reframe their maladaptive values when they are around individuals and families that exhibit a more positive way of life.

Become involved in your local schools, in local non-profit groups, and in church organizations. Perhaps the local soup kitchen for the disadvantaged would appreciate your family's help. I know of one retired gentleman who goes to an elementary school once a week to help the very young children read. As you do these things, the neighborhood will notice. As you do these things with joy and happiness, the community will want a taste of it as well.

Please take the recommendations that are listed in the previous chapter and apply them to activities within the community. It is indeed contagious in a very healthy way.

— CHAPTER 44 —

HEALING THE NATION

As I mentioned earlier in this book, a team of horses offer greater strength and tenacity that a single steed. As we attempt to offset the negative impact of *Delusional Entitlement Disorder*, we use that theory by taking the model for the family and expanding it within the neighborhood and community.

When communities transfer their positive energy to a larger population, it makes the region and nation a better place. When something is positive, energetic, compassionate and healthy; it attracts others.

Individuals who have developed a resiliency to *D.E.D.* by cultivating healthy behaviors and attitude, stand out within communities in a very dynamic way. Many of us have observed someone starting a cause or event at a local level with a great vision. Others around them want to be a part of that energy. Soon that individual is making a positive impact on larger populations within their region. Before long stewardship and focus on something beside one's self has spread like wildfire. *D.E.D.* becomes less prevalent where healthy and healing experiences exist.

Here is an example of the opposite of *Delusional Entitlement Disorder.* Approximately thirty years ago, a small boy was fighting for his life in the battle against cancer. A law officer in the locality of the young boy had befriended the youngster and his family. The ill young man had always dreamed of being a police officer. Realizing the gravity of the young boy's declining health, the local officer began recruiting the efforts of his colleagues. Knowing the young man's condition, the officer had promised him an opportunity to ride along with other public safety officers in the community. Within days, volunteers had constructed an official uniform for the boy and made provisions for him to take his ride.

Several people, abandoning their own agenda and putting their own wants and needs on the back burner, came together in a volunteer force to make the wish of this very ill boy come true.

The young man lost his battle with cancer shortly after the experience. But for a short while, his magic wish brought a smile, joy and laughter to his frail body.

But the story doesn't end there. From one family and one community the word spread. Other communities wanting to form a similar function for children with life-threatening illness became a reality. From the communities, the volunteer effort expanded nationally. Currently there are literally tens of thousands of volunteers for this nationally-based wish granting organization that put the stewardship of ill children before their own needs (*for more information, pleases visit www.wish.org*). These incredible people grant a wish for a child with a life-threatening illness every 40 minutes throughout the country.

From the stewardship and compassion of one family, communities were touched and a nation was brought together for a cause.

Where this type of spirit exists, **D.E.D**. finds it very difficult to plant its feet.

Were we as a nation able to serve soup to those who are hungry, repair the tire for the stranded lady, buy Christmas gifts for the disadvantaged, learn to adapt to our disabilities, appreciate the small gifts in life, learn to know our neighbors, celebrate patriotism, participate in charitable events, enjoin others in a sense of positive unity, welcome those that are different in culture than we, share out faith by example, teach our children well, and honor our parents more deeply there wouldn't be a place for **Delusional Entitlement Disorder** to grow.

— CHAPTER 45- —

A DAILY PRESCRIPTION TO AVOID D.E.D.

- Arise early and give thanks for the day in whatever manner you feel comfortable.
- Be grateful for the blessings you have around you. If you can't see blessings, take a few more minutes and search for them.
- Greet those around you with a kind and gentle gratitude.
- Eat healthy. Avoid junk food.
- Demand less and give more to those have very little.
- Focus on someone else more than yourself.
- Strive for a home, worksite and community of structure and purpose instead of chaos.
- Read more inspirational articles.
- Focus less on how others can serve you and increase your concentration on how you can help others.
- Treat others like you would enjoy being treated.
- Invest energy into your community.
- Teach others how to be healthier.
- Strive to engage in no activity that would embarrass you should you have to explain

yourself to your family, your doctor, your
lawyer, your clergy, a court of law, yourself or
God.

Made in the USA
Lexington, KY
15 March 2010